Sound Doctrine: Innocent of the Blood of Any of You

Understanding Paul's Charge to Timothy, Titus, the Elders of Ephesus, and Apostolic Church Teachers Today in Light of 2 Timothy 4:3

Copyright 2025

Les Moore

Forward..3

Prolegomenon..6

Sound Doctrine..9

The Charge of Sound Doctrine........................13

The Gospel of the Kingdom of God................21

Salvation and the Sound Doctrine of Paul....40

Foundational Principle Doctrines of Christ...50

    Repentance...50

    Faith Towards God......................................51

    Baptisms..52

    Laying On Of Hands...................................92

    Resurrection of the Dead.........................93

    Eternal Judgment.......................................95

The Resurrection Power of Jesus Christ.......97

Jesus is God..101

The Revelation of Jesus Christ......................135

Fulfillment..150

Conclusion of the Whole Matter...................155

Biography...169

† Forward and Dedication

I am a Christian theologian. Theology is the study of God, classically the science that allowed us to understand all other sciences. I am also a naturopathic physician and acupuncturist, believing that all healing comes from God, but the Lord said the sick need a 'physician', which a word coined by Hippocrates meaning 'one who uses nature.' As an acupuncturist, I want to be extremely accurate in the placement of my needles, otherwise it would be approxipuncture (maybe the point is approximately there, maybe not; maybe my theology is correct, maybe not). As a systematic theologian, I want my theology to be accurate also, precise to be exact, otherwise I am off course. I do know that my theology and understanding of the revelation of Scripture and what the Lord is asking me to do changes over time. Still yet, I do not want to be sloppy and inaccurate in my theology or understanding what the Lord is asking me to do, and neither does anyone. Now, if one happens to be off theologically, it is okay scripturally to be off on an understanding of God's plan somewhat, as Peter still thought eight years later after he had received the Holy Spirit and was healing lame people that he couldn't go into the house of an unclean believer at Cornelius' house, and James still thought that Paul had to do a Nazarite ritual to appease the Jews when he came back from his missionary trip (Paul was willing to do it to not stumble anyone), and Paul writes to the Galatians in chapter 2 that Peter, James, Barnabus, and many others were off in their understanding of the Word of God. But, we want to be precise and do the exact will of God, not our own will or the will of our denomination or follow the doctrines of men.

I am not going to judge if someone is saved or not- Jesus will do that; but I am going to point to what the Scriptures say about salvation from a holistic understanding of the totality of Scripture, not a reductionist interpretation of a single Scripture or a tradition of man.

Much of what we uncover in the Scriptures during this dissection of Paul's charge to the elders of Ephesus will be shocking to what I or others have understood theology to be, but we must be honest with what the plan of salvation is and who is it that will be saving us and judging us. That we will be judged by Jesus is clear. What we will be judged on is clear also.

God's plan of salvation is laid out accurately and clearly in Acts 2:38 and repeated through the Book of Acts and the Epistles, although it contradicts later historical theology and most contemporary theology and church doctrine. The structure of the Church is laid out by God in 1 Corinthians 12:28 clearly, although most churches do not operate in the order that God has created, but that is covered in my book *Operational Ministry: The Structure and Operations of the Church and Functional Roles of Church Officers*. This book is dedicated to the Church triumphant and victorious, to whom the gates of hell shall not prevail, and to my wife and daughters, who are a part of the bride of Christ, and to the memory of Bishop G. L. Akers Sanford, NC, who fed me the pure

Word of God for over a decade of Christian spiritual formation.

Les Moore, MAAT, D.Min.

Feast of Dedication, 2025

† Prolegomenon

In the presence of God and of Christ Jesus, Who will judge the living and the dead, and in view of His appearing and His kingdom, **I give you this charge: Preach** *the word; be prepared in season and out of season; correct, rebuke and encourage—with great patience and careful instruction. For the time will come when people will not put up with* **sound doctrine**. *Instead, to suit their own desires, they will gather around them a great number of teachers to say what their itching ears want to hear. They will turn their ears away from the truth and turn aside to myths. But you, keep your head in all situations, endure hardship, do the work of an evangelist, discharge all the duties of your ministry* (2 Timothy 4:1-5)

But as for you, **teach** *what accords with* **sound doctrine** (Titus 2:1).

We also know that the law is made not for the righteous but for lawbreakers and rebels, the ungodly and sinful, the unholy and irreligious, for those who kill their fathers or mothers, for murderers, for the sexually immoral, for those practicing homosexuality, for slave traders and liars and perjurers—and for whatever else is contrary to the **sound doctrine** *that conforms to the gospel concerning the glory of the blessed God, which he entrusted to me* (1 Timothy 1:9-11).

He must hold firmly to the trustworthy message as it has been taught, so that he can encourage others by **sound doctrine** *and refute those who oppose it* (Titus 1:9).

*And they continued steadfastly in the **apostles' doctrine** and fellowship, and in breaking of bread, and in prayers* (Acts 2:42).

*Watch your life and **doctrine** closely. **Persevere** in them, because if you do, **you will save both yourself and your hearers*** (1 Timothy 4:16).

What I am going to examine in this book is the **sound doctrine** that Paul was charging the early church with in the book of Acts and in his epistles. Although almost all that I share is scriptural evidence, most contemporary theologians and Christians will be shocked at what the scriptures say about sound doctrine, resulting in rejection, rebellion, disobedience, and cries of heresy, even though the doctrine that I am teaching is what Paul, Peter, Jesus, and the rest of the apostles were martyred for.

Yes, martyred for. Jesus was crucified for claiming to be God. Stephen was martyred for preaching Jesus Christ. Paul was willing to die for the Name of Jesus.

I am only interested in truth. Belief doesn't count for anything. People believe all kinds of doctrine, but there can only be one truth. Jesus said that He was the Way, the Truth, and the Life. So what is the truth that we find in the Scriptures, void of the doctrines of men and vain philosophies? The truth can be found by dissecting the sound doctrine that Paul said he taught the Ephesians.

What you read in this book will shock your understanding of soteriology (the study of salvation) and sound doctrine, making some feel actual sickness and others great anger. Although it may be counter to contemporary understanding of salvation and theology, it is exactly what the New Covenant teaches and what many teachers taught throughout history about the nature of God and salvation, and most were martyred, exiled, excommunicated, or imprisoned for their belief.

What I am teaching is basic Christianity as taught by the apostles according to the written word of God. And although the reader may find it shocking and against all their understanding of Christianity, it is the same understanding that Jesus taught, His apostles taught, some early church fathers taught, and what important modern theologians believed, which I will demonstrate through this text and at the conclusion.

† Sound Doctrine: The Doctrine of Jesus is Pure

Doctrine, from the Latin *'docere'*, means 'teaching' or 'to teach.' It is the same root word from where we get our word 'doctor' from, meaning 'teacher' (of health in the case of medicine). Jesus explicitly declares that His doctrine is pure in John 7:

My doctrine is not from Myself: it comes from the One who sent Me; and if anyone is prepared to do His will, he will know whether my doctrine is from God or whether my doctrine is My own. When a person's doctrine is his own, he is hoping for honor for himself; but when he is working for the glory of one who sent him, then he is sincere and by no means a false teacher. Did not Moses give you the law? And yet not one of you keeps the Law! (John 7:16-19)

This is a warning from the Lord that we are not seeking God's honor alone, but we are seeking our own glory and advantage. The cause for this self-seeking glory and pride is the distance between God's will and ours. Whenever we give up our will completely, we will receive in return from God so completely and so truly God's will that it becomes our own will. There has completed an exchange of wills between God and us. If our will is God's will, it is good; but if God's will becomes our will, it is far better. The God of the Kingdom of God is not your God until that same God exchanges wills with you. We must let go of our will and our denominational pride and listen to the will of God. This is why we must give up everything for the Kingdom of God, especially our own self-will. As long as we hold on to some part of our own self-will, we have not entered into the Kingdom of God. But whosoever can let go of themselves and their own self-will will find it easy to relinquish all material things and all false doctrines attached to the pride of knowledge.

Sound Doctrine

*For the time will come when people will not put up with **sound doctrine**. Instead, to suit their own desires, they will gather around them a great number of teachers to say what their itching ears want to hear.* (2 Timothy 4:3)

Sound doctrine is teaching the scriptures more accurately that produces wholeness, healing, and salvation. Unsound doctrine would be teaching that produces division and leads to death. Sound doctrine makes us whole. Sound doctrine reconciles us to God, healing that divide that is caused by sin, rebellion, and disobedience. Paul told the elders of Ephesus in Acts 20 that that time of false teachers would come immediately after he left.

*We have heard that some **teachers** went out from us **without our authorization** and disturbed you, troubling your minds by what they said.* (Acts 15:24)

It didn't take long before false doctrine began to be taught in the early church in the book of Acts. James calls those who taught the Gentiles that they had to keep the law **unauthorized teachers**. If there are unauthorized teachers who teach false doctrine, then we need to understand what authorized teachers are and what sound doctrine is.

Teaching unbiblical and unsound doctrine can happen to the best of us, even authorized teachers such as Peter and Barnabus. We see in the letter to the Galatians that Paul points out that Peter, Barnabus, James, and others were teaching things to itching ears that were not sound doctrine that we see Biblically.

*When Cephas (Peter) came to Antioch, I opposed him to his face, because **he stood condemned**. For **before certain men came from James**, he used to eat with the Gentiles. But when they arrived, **he began to draw back and separate himself from the Gentiles because he was afraid of those who belonged to the circumcision group**. The other Jews joined him in his hypocrisy, so that by their hypocrisy **even Barnabas was led astray**. When I saw that **they were not acting in line with the truth of the Gospel**, I said to Cephas in front of them all, "You are a Jew, yet you live like a Gentile and not like a Jew. How is it, then, that you force Gentiles to follow Jewish customs? (Galatians 2:11-14).*

As we can observe here, James sent men to Peter, misunderstanding what the Lord wanted the Church to do and become, and had them pulling away from the Gentiles. This was because there was a party or denomination within the believers that thought circumcision and the following of the law was necessary for salvation. This false doctrine was able to influence and put fear into Peter, other Jewish believers in Jesus, and even Barnabus, until the Lord sent Paul to teach them sound doctrine, and this **sound doctrine must be in alignment with the Truth of the Gospel**.

This Truth is what we are searching for and teaching. It can only come from authorized teachers who are in submission and obedient and must reflect the Gospel of the Kingdom of God.

† The Charge of Sound Doctrine

The Greek word translated as 'sound' is *hugieia*, the same root where we get the word 'hygiene' from. *Hugieia* is the Greek god of healing, and is a word chosen by the Holy Spirit of God to define teaching that brings wholeness and salvation. (Do not fear that it is a worldly word, as Christ overcame the world. We have Saints in the scriptures that are named after false gods and continue to use those names in the scriptures, such as Apollos, Epaphroditus, and Dionysius.) *Hugieia* (or *Hygieia/Hygeia*) is the Ancient Greek word for health, and refers to the Greek goddess of health, cleanliness, and hygiene, daughter of Asclepius, the god of medicine, whose name directly gives us the English word "hygiene". She represents the prevention of sickness, promoting wellness, and is often depicted with a serpent and a bowl, symbolizing healing and the continuity of good health. *Hygieia* personifies physical well-being, cleanliness, and sanitation in Greek mythology, focusing on preventive health rather than just curing illness. As the daughter of Asclepius, the god of medicine, she's part of the divine family of healing, alongside sisters like Panacea (universal remedy) and Iaso (recuperation; this is also the root of the Greek word Jesus uses for 'physician.') Her common attributes are a serpent (representing healing) and a cup or bowl, symbolizing medicine or transformation. Her name is the direct root of the English word "hygiene," making her a constant reminder of healthy practices. In essence, Hygieia embodies the proactive aspects of health—staying clean, eating well, exercising, and preventing disease, making her a timeless figure in medicine and wellness. This is the word that the Holy Spirit used to put before the word 'doctrine' in **sound doctrine, meaning teaching that makes you whole, healed, and restored.**

In the Epistles to Timothy, Paul sent Timothy to Ephesus to oversee the churches in Ephesus and charged him to teach **sound doctrine**. Scholars believe there were more than one hundred thousand believers in Ephesus, one of the largest cities in the world, at this time. The Epistles of Timothy and Titus have been called 'pastoral epistles' for a couple centuries. This is incorrect, in that they are 'apostolic epistles,' where Timothy was apostolically overseeing the churches in Ephesus and Titus was sent to Crete to ordain elders and establish order in the cities of Crete, which had between 30 to 100 cities on the island, making it an apostolic mission also.

What could be the sound doctrine that he was instructing Timothy to teach? Was it anything we want it to be? Was it what our denominations and seminaries and Bible colleges taught us? Was it what scholarly theologians and doctors of the Church have written over the centuries? Was it what we see on social media today? The Bible tells us what Paul was teaching at Ephesus, and it is as accurate and clear as can be and is backed up by the teaching of Jesus, Peter, John, Philip, and the Scriptures.

He (Apollos) began to speak boldly in the synagogue. When Priscilla and Aquila heard him, they invited him to their home and **taught him the Way of God more accurately**. *(Acts 18:26)*

In Acts 18 at Ephesus we see Priscilla and her husband Aquila pull Apollos (one of the 25 named apostles in the New Testament) to their home and teach him the Way of God **more accurately**. He was a powerful preacher and was teaching Jesus and the Way of the Lord accurately, but Priscilla and Aquila taught him the Way of God **more accurately**.

Meanwhile a Jew named Apollos, a native of Alexandria, came to Ephesus. He was a learned man, with a thorough knowledge of the Scriptures. He had been instructed in the Way of the Lord, and he spoke with great fervor and taught about Jesus accurately, though he knew only the baptism of John. (Acts 18:24-25)

<u>Apollos</u>

- Trained, learned man
- Thorough knowledge of the Scriptures
- Instructed in the Way of the Lord
- Spoke with great fervor
- Taught about Jesus accurately
- Spoke boldly in the synagogue

Priscilla and Aquila taught him the Way of God **more accurately** because he only knew the baptism of John, not the baptism of Jesus. This is a significant teaching in the Book of Acts and is critical for understanding what the will of God is. As we will see, we are talking about both the water baptism in the Name of Jesus and the baptism in the Holy Spirt.

He had been instructed in the Way of the Lord, and he spoke with great fervor and taught about Jesus accurately, though **he knew only the baptism of John**. (Acts 18:25)

We find immediately after this in Acts 19 that Paul encounters twelve believers in Ephesus who only knew the baptism of John (which is in water and of repentance), and he **REBAPTIZES** them in the **Name of Jesus** (in water) and lays hands on them to be filled with the Holy Spirit and speak with tongues as the initial evidence of the infilling of the Holy Spirit (in all incidences of the receiving of the Holy Spirit in the book of Acts) and prophesying. (In all occasions of the infilling of the Holy Spirit in the book of Acts the believers spoke in tongues, prophesized, and/or magnified God. This is how Peter was able to see that those at Cornelius' house were filled with the Holy Spirit, the way Simon the Sorcerer was able to want to buy the gift, the way the Jews could see that the disciples were filled on the day of Pentecost, and the way that Paul knew these Ephesians were filled with the Holy Spirit. It is something that others can observe. It is an observable manifestation, contrary to historical church teaching.)

These disciples in Ephesus believed in Jesus and had been baptized wrongly into John, and Paul taught them

more accurately about Jesus and **the Way of God, which is the path to salvation: Repent, be Baptized in the Name of Jesus, and Filled with the Holy Spirit.**

Both of these examples of Apollos and the disciples at **Ephesus** being soundly corrected by Priscilla, Aquila, and Paul, demonstrate to us that we are to lead people into **full obedience** of God's plan for the New Testament church, not just partial obedience. Since Scripture shows us what Paul was teaching and applying at Ephesus, we know what sound doctrine he was charging Timothy with.

*We have heard that some **teachers** went out from us **without our authorization** and disturbed you, troubling your minds by what they said.* (Acts 15:24)

Sound doctrine does not mean teaching anything that you want. We see the apostles in Acts, under the leadership of James, send out a letter telling the church that 'unauthorized teachers' have been teaching them wrongly. We see the scriptures warn us to 'rightly divide the word of God,' and if there is a right way to divide the Word of God then there is a wrong way to divide the Word of God. We see in Acts 19 that Apollos (named as one of the 25 named apostles in the New Testament) was teaching the Word of God and about Jesus accurately, but Priscilla and Aquila pulled him aside and taught him the Word of God more accurately. We also see in the scriptures that those who teach will be judged harder.

Not many of you should become teachers, my brothers, for you know that we who teach will be judged with greater strictness (James 3:1).

James warns prospective teachers of greater accountability because their words have significant influence, meaning teachers will be held to a higher standard for the truth they convey, as Jesus explained in Luke 12:48:

For everyone to whom much is given, much will be required, and from him to whom they entrusted much, more will be demanded (Luke 12:48).

Teachers are judged more strictly due to the greater responsibility of influencing others' understanding of God's Word. The context of the passage immediately following highlights the power and danger of the tongue (James 3:2-12), suggesting that teachers who misuse their speech or teach error face harsher judgment for misleading people. In Ezekiel 3:17-18 and 33:7-9, God warns prophets that they are responsible for the people's lives if they fail to warn them. This is why Paul states to the Ephesian elders that he is **innocent of their blood because he has taught them the truth of Jesus and the Gospel of the Kingdom in sound doctrine**.

The Apostles' Doctrine

The only time that we see the word 'doctrine' in the scriptures combined with 'apostles', meaning apostolic doctrine, is in Acts 2:42, where 'they continued in apostolic doctrine.' What the apostles were teaching in the Scriptures is the doctrine that we continue today to be truly 'apostolic', as opposed to apostolic succession or apostolic titles, which are both popular today in old church structures and newer denominational movements. We know what doctrine Peter was teaching right before this that the church was to continue in, and was verified by the assenting eleven apostles standing with him that day and continued in the teachings of Stephen, Philip, Paul, and others.

Today, I see entire denominations and movements teaching that there are three separate entities in the Godhead, outrightly teaching tritheism (not looking at the Trinity as One), if not just plain polytheism, and some teaching that Jesus in not God, when none of the scriptures point to this; they only point to the oneness of God, who <u>manifested Himself</u> (Jesus) in the flesh and poured out His Spirit (Holy Spirit) upon us with the <u>manifestation of the Spirit</u>. The being and acts of the Father and the Son are one and not divided. This is the *homoousion*, same substance/essence, one in being, and is the central doctrine of Christianity. This truth of the Gospel entirely depends on the homoousion, the unity or oneness of the Son with the Father (...until we all come in the unity of the faith...as Paul writes to the Ephesians). The life and work of Jesus Christ are intrinsic to the very being of God. In Him, it is truly God's being and acts as a human.

I see entire denominations and most written literature and most internet information and social media claiming that salvation comes by mental assent only, when the scriptures are clear that one must repent, be baptized in the Name of Jesus for the forgiveness of sins, be filled with the Holy Spirit, and abide in His Body (live in Christ).

God has charged me by the laying on of hands and through prophecy to teach Sound Doctrine, and this book is written to rebuke, correct, and outright reject any false doctrine, false teachers, unauthorized teachers, doctrines of men, and doctrines of demons. **We are to lead believers to full obedience of God's plan for the New Testament Church, not partial obedience**. That is what a teacher is to do- ground one in the Word of God in order to become obedient to His commands.

Before we move on to what Sound Doctrine that Paul was teaching, we need to understand what the Gospel is first, since this is the milieu in which Sound Doctrine exists.

† The Gospel of the Kingdom of God

The Gospel, or Good News, that Jesus, Peter, Paul, and Philip taught, was the Gospel of the Kingdom of God, which is here, now, at hand, within, and future. This is the first message Jesus taught and the Gospel that He continued to teach to the Jews throughout His earthly ministry. It is the Gospel that Philip taught to the Samaritans and it is the Gospel that Paul taught to the Gentiles. The Good News is that the Kingdom of God is now within us, individually and as the body of Christ. God's domain is within us, and His dominion is in our lives!

Paul Preached the Kingdom of God:

***Proclaiming the Kingdom of God** and teaching about the Lord Jesus Christ with all boldness and without hindrance.* (Acts 28:31)

We see that Paul was preaching the Kingdom of God and teaching about the Lord Jesus Christ. This is what Paul said he was doing the whole time he was ministering. This is important to understand when we are trying to see what sound doctrine he was charging the elders of Ephesus, Timothy, Titus, and the apostolic churches he wrote epistles to.

Jesus Preached the Gospel of the Kingdom of God:

*Now after John was put in prison, Jesus came to Galilee, **preaching the Gospel of the Kingdom of God,** and saying, "The time is fulfilled, and the **Kingdom of God** is at hand. **Repent, and believe in the Gospel**."* (Mark 1:14-15)

Jesus was not teaching a salvation message- He is salvation. He was teaching a Kingdom message. He stated that the Good News was the Kingdom of God and that the time and all prophecy was fulfilled, therefore we must repent (change our hearts, minds, turn to God) and believe in the Gospel. What Gospel? The Gospel of the Kingdom of God! If one does not believe that the time is fulfilled and the Kingdom of God is here, then they do not believe.

*And He said to them, "Truly, I say to you, there are some standing here who will not taste death until they **see the Kingdom of God** after it has come with power." (Mark 9:1)*

Jesus told those listening to Him that some would still be alive when the Kingdom of God had come in power, which happened on the day of Pentecost when the Holy Spirit came upon them, which was power from on high.

Jesus Came to Preach the Gospel of the Kingdom of God:

*But He said to them, "I must **preach the Gospel of the Kingdom of God** to the other towns also, because **that is why I was sent.**" (Luke 4:43)*

Jesus says that His mission is to preach and proclaim the Good News of the Kingdom of God, which is here, now, within, at hand, and future. This is Jesus in His own Holy words.

The Apostles Knew He Preached and Brought the Gospel of the Kingdom of God:

*Now it came to pass, afterward, that He went through every city and village, **preaching and bringing the Gospel of the Kingdom of God. And the twelve were with Him**.* (Luke 8:1)

The apostles were with Jesus and knew what He was preaching and bringing the Kingdom of God, and this shaped everything they did in the future. They also preached the Kingdom of God and how to enter into it.

Jesus Told His Disciples to 'Go and Preach the Kingdom of God':

*And Jesus said to him, "Leave the dead to bury their own dead. But as for you, **go and proclaim the Kingdom of God**."* (Luke 9:60)

It is easy to see that Jesus told them to go and minister by proclaiming the Kingdom of God to everyone they ministered to. This is significantly different than most ministry today.

Jesus told the Disciples What They are to Say:

*After this the Lord appointed seventy-two others and sent them two by two ahead of Him to every town and place where He was about to go....Heal the sick who are there, and **say to them, 'The Kingdom of God has come upon you.'*** (Luke 10:1,9)

After Jesus instructed the twelve to preach the Kingdom of God, He then instructed the total seventy-two disciples (theologically known as apostles since they are sent ones, which is why the Orthodox Church says there were seventy-two apostles in Scripture) to proclaim that the Kingdom of God has come upon you when you are healed in the Name of Jesus.

It is the Father's Pleasure to Give Us the Kingdom:

*Fear not, little flock, for **it is your Father's good pleasure to give you the Kingdom**. Sell your possessions, and give to the needy. Provide yourselves with moneybags that do not grow old, with a treasure in the heavens that does not fail, where no thief approaches and no moth destroys. For where your treasure is, there will your heart be also.* (Luke 12:32-34)

Although it is His good pleasure to give us the Kingdom, He wants us to give up everything for it, as He tells us in multiple parables. He says that our heart should be in the Kingdom of God.

Today the Gospel of the Kingdom of God is Preached:

*The Law and the Prophets were proclaimed until John. **Since that time, the Gospel of the Kingdom of God is being preached**, and everyone is forcing their way into it.* (Luke 16:16)

Up until John the Baptist, the Law and the Prophets were proclaimed. Since the time of John the Baptist, two thousand years ago, the Gospel of the Kingdom of God is preached, and everyone is pressing into it. Why are some teaching and preaching something other than the Kingdom of God and how to enter it? Why do some teach the Law and the works thereof?

The Kingdom of God is Within You!

Being asked by the Pharisees when the Kingdom of God would come, He answered them, "The Kingdom of God is not coming in ways that can be observed, nor will they say, 'Look, here it is!' or 'There!' for behold, **the Kingdom of God is within you.***"* (Luke 17:20-21)

Many false teachers teach that the Kingdom of God is only coming in the future, but Jesus clearly teaches that the Kingdom of God is within, it is His domain within you and His dominion in your life. It comes when someone is healed in the Name of Jesus. It comes when you submit in obedience to Jesus. The Kingdom of God, His domain and dominion, are within the obedient believer. Do not look for the Kingdom of God somewhere else or at a different time, but look within when you have believed, repented, been baptized in His Name, and filled with His Holy Spirit.

You Must be Born Again to See the Kingdom of God:

Jesus answered him, "Truly, truly, I say to you, unless one is born again he cannot **see the Kingdom of God.***"* (John 3:3)

You must be born again, of water and Spirit, in order to **SEE** the Kingdom of God. This allows us the revelation of being able to see that we are operating in the Kingdom of God.

Jesus answered, Verily, verily, I say unto you, Except a man be born of water and of the Spirit, he cannot **enter into the Kingdom of God.** (John 3:5)

One must be born again of water (water baptism) and of the Spirit (infilling of the Holy Spirit of God) in order to **SEE** and **ENTER** the Kingdom of God.

We are to Pray for the Kingdom to Come!

*Pray then like this: "Our Father in heaven, hallowed be Your Name. **Your Kingdom come**, Your will be done, on earth as it is in heaven." (Matthew 6:9-10)*

We are to actively pray for the Kingdom to come, which is His will, as we see Paul describe in Acts 20 when he says:

*Now I know that none of you among whom I have gone about **preaching the Kingdom** will ever see me again. Therefore, **I declare** to you today that **I am innocent of the blood of any of you**. For I have **not hesitated to proclaim to you the whole WILL of God** (Acts 20:25-27).*

We are to Seek First His Kingdom

*But **seek first His Kingdom** and His righteousness, and all these things will be given to you as well. (Matthew 6:33)*

First thing in the morning, first thing in decisions, first thing in business, first thing in family and marriage, is to seek His Kingdom. Our desire is to seek His face and to know Him. To know Him is to know His Kingdom, therefore we are to seek primarily His Kingdom, along with His righteousness, which He has given us because it is required to be in His Kingdom and His Holy Spirit convicts us of our righteousness.

The Kingdom is Here, Now, At Hand, Within, and Yet!

*I tell you, many will come from the east and the west and will take their places at the feast with Abraham, Isaac and Jacob in **the Kingdom of Heaven**.* (Matthew 8:11)

The Kingdom is future also, when we will sit down at the feast. There is no difference between the terms Kingdom of Heaven and Kingdom of God, because we see in the Gospels that the phrase is used interchangeably in exactly the same situations.

Jesus Preached the Gospel of the Kingdom and Healing is a Part of It!

*And Jesus went throughout all the cities and villages, teaching in their synagogues **and preaching the Gospel of the Kingdom and healing** every disease and every affliction.* (Matthew 9:35)

Healing is a part of the Kingdom of God and healing is a sign of believers. Healing comes with those who believe in the Lord Jesus Christ and have submitted to his commands and entered His Kingdom. The laying on of hands and healing in the Name of Jesus is a sign that one is a follower and believer in Jesus Christ and a believer in His healing power.

Deliverance is a Part of the Kingdom of God!

*But if it is by the Spirit of God that I drive out demons, then **the Kingdom of God has come upon you**.* (Matthew 12:28)

If you have been delivered from any oppression or bondage, the Kingdom of God has come upon you.

*He said to them, "Go into all the world **and preach the Gospel** to all creation. **Whoever believes and is baptized will be saved**, but whoever does not believe will be condemned. And these signs will accompany those who believe: **In My Name they will cast out demons**; they will speak in new tongues; they will pick up snakes with their hands; and when they drink deadly poison, it will not hurt them at all; **they will lay their hands on sick people, and they will get well**."* (Mark 16:15-18)

This Gospel in Mark 16:15 is the Gospel of the Kingdom of God, which is the Gospel we are to preach. Those who believe, have repented, and are baptized in the Name of Jesus will also be accompanied by signs of healing and deliverance.

Many theologians and church leaders don't teach the latter half of Mark 16, saying it is not in the scriptures. There are 1837 ancient manuscripts that have the verses above and only 3 that do not! This is what Jesus said.

The Kingdom Continues to Expand!

***The Kingdom of Heaven** is like a mustard seed, which a man took and planted in his field. Though it is the smallest of all seeds, yet **when it grows, it is the largest** of garden plants and becomes a tree, so that the birds come and perch in its branches.* (Matthew 13:31-32)

The Kingdom Grows!

*He told them another parable. "**The Kingdom of Heaven** is like leaven that a woman took and hid in three measures of flour, till it was all leavened."* (Matthew 12:33)

There is Joy in the Kingdom!

The Kingdom of Heaven *is like treasure hidden in a field, which a man found and covered up. Then in his **joy** he goes and sells all that he has and buys that field.* (Matthew 13:44)

There are many believers who do not have joy. If you are in the Kingdom of God, you have joy! Paul tells the Thessalonians to 'Rejoice always!' Paul had to repeat it to the Philippians who were having some disagreements within the deacons at Philippi. *Rejoice in the Lord always; again I will say, rejoice!* (Philippians 4:4). The repetition of 'rejoice' highlights that joy in God isn't conditional but a continuous state of being that we are in in the Kingdom. This true joy is found 'in the Lord,' focusing on His goodness and presence, not external situations, but the fact that we are in His Kingdom with the presence of His Holy Spirit.

We are to Give Up Everything for the Kingdom!

Again, ***the Kingdom of Heaven*** *is like a merchant in search of fine pearls, who, on finding one pearl of great value, went and sold all that he had and bought it.* (Matthew 13:45-46)

*Again, **the Kingdom of Heaven** is like a net that was thrown into the sea and gathered fish of every kind. When it was full, men drew it ashore and sat down and sorted the good into containers but threw away the bad. So it will be at the end of the age. The angels will come out and separate the evil from the righteous and throw them into the fiery furnace. In that place there will be weeping and gnashing of teeth.* (Matthew 13:47-50)

There will be those that will be separated out of the Kingdom at the end of the age. This will include false prophets, false apostles, false teachers, unauthorized teachers, and those that are in the lists from Paul and Peter and John that say they will not inherit the Kingdom, such as murderers, the sexually immoral, slanderers, gossipers, liars, etc. Repent, or you will die, Peter tells Simon the Sorcerer.

We are to be Instruments of Righteousness in the Kingdom of God!

*Do not offer any part of yourself to sin as an instrument of wickedness, but rather offer yourselves to God as those who have been brought from death to life; and **offer every part of yourself to Him as an instrument of righteousness*** (Romans 6:13).

You are an instrument of righteousness in the hands of God, therefore we are to offer ourselves to Him and be holy as He is holy.

We are Given the Keys of the Kingdom!

*Jesus says to Peter, "I will give you **the keys of the Kingdom of Heaven**, and whatever you bind on earth* *shall be bound in heaven, and whatever you loose on earth shall be loosed in heaven."* (Matthew 16:9)

We will examine the keys that He gave Peter later in this book.

The Kingdom of God will be given to a people producing its fruits.

*Therefore I tell you, **the Kingdom of God** will be taken away from you and given to a people producing its **fruits**.* (Matthew 21:43)

The Gospel of the Kingdom will be Preached Everywhere!

*And this **Gospel of the Kingdom will be proclaimed throughout the whole world** as a testimony to all nations, and then the end will come.* (Matthew 24:14)

The Gospel of the Kingdom of God, which is here, now, at hand, within, and future, will be preached throughout the whole world before the end of time comes.

*When the Son of Man comes in His glory, and all the angels with Him, then He will sit on His glorious throne. Before Him will be gathered all the nations, and He will separate people one from another as a shepherd separates the sheep from the goats. And He will place the sheep on his right, but the goats on the left. Then the King will say to those on his right, "Come, you who are blessed by my Father, **inherit the Kingdom** prepared for you from the foundation of the world. For I was hungry and you gave me food, I was thirsty and you* *gave me drink, I was a stranger and you welcomed me, I was naked and you clothed me, I was sick and you visited me, I was in prison and you came to me."* (Matthew 25:31-36)

Those who have served the Lord and loved their neighbor as themselves, feeding, clothing, welcoming, and visiting in their affliction, will inherit the Kingdom of God.

Paul Preached the Kingdom of God!

Then Paul dwelt two whole years in his own rented house, and received all who came to him, **preaching the Kingdom of God** *and teaching the things which concern the Lord Jesus Christ with all confidence, no one forbidding him.* (Acts 28:30-31)

After Paul was run out of various places by various disobedient people and eventually imprisoned, God placed him in one place and had many seekers of God come to him and he preached to them about the Kingdom of God and the Lord Jesus Christ.

This is interesting, in that when people rebelled against Paul's teaching, the Lord allowed him to be imprisoned and teach out of his house, as opposed to traveling and teaching at synagogues and from house to house. God places us where He wants us to minister from, and it may not necessarily be what we like or want.

Jesus Taught the Kingdom of God for Forty Days after His Resurrection

*After His suffering, He presented Himself to them and gave many convincing proofs that He was alive. He appeared to them over a period of forty days **and spoke about the Kingdom of God**.* (Acts 1:3)

Jesus taught His disciples, including the apostles, the Gospel of the Kingdom of God for three years, then, after His resurrection, came back and taught them the Gospel of the Kingdom of God for forty more days, ensuring they understood His message and His Way. This is how important God considers the message of the Gospel of the Kingdom of God.

The Kingdom is Righteousness, Peace and Joy in the Holy Spirit!

*For **the Kingdom of God** is not a matter of eating and drinking but of **righteousness and peace and joy in the Holy Spirit**.* (Romans 14:17)

The Kingdom of God is the King's Domain and Dominion in your life, where the Holy Spirit of God now tabernacles within us, and it is righteousness, peace, and joy. Jesus is our righteousness, Jesus is our peace, and Jesus is our joy.

We are created in His image, which is righteousness and holiness.

*And put on the **new self**, which **in the likeness of God** has been **created in righteousness and holiness of the truth**.* (Ephesians 4:24)

The new self is the image of God that we were created in, and that image is righteousness and holiness of the truth. There is a Holy Truth, and Jesus is the Truth. What we think or believe is not necessarily the truth, but we are to seek the truth. Jesus' teaching and what He allowed the apostles to write in Scripture is truth.

The Kingdom Must be Taken by Force

*From the days of John the Baptist until now the **Kingdom of Heaven** has suffered violence, and the **violent take it by force**.* (Matthew 11:12)

*The Law and the Prophets were proclaimed until John. Since that time, the **Gospel of the Kingdom of God** is being preached, and everyone is forcing their way into it* (Luke 16:16).

Everyone is pressing into the Kingdom of God. The enemy wants to stop us from entering and seeing the Kingdom of God.

The Kingdom of God is Power!

*For the **Kingdom of God** does not consist in word but in **power**.* (1 Corinthians 4:20)

The Kingdom of God is not just talk and words, it consists of power. Debates, social media arguments, denominational condemnation, intellectualism, mental assent, dead words and dead works, none of this is the Kingdom of God. That is all stubble. The Kingdom of God consists of power- power over death, power over the enemy, power of the Holy Spirit and all the gifts of God, which is power from on high.

*Or do you not know that the **unrighteous will not inherit the Kingdom of God**? Do not be deceived: **neither** the sexually immoral, nor idolaters, nor adulterers, nor men who practice homosexuality, nor thieves, nor the greedy, nor drunkards, nor revilers, nor swindlers **will inherit the Kingdom of God**.* (1 Corinthians 6:9-10)

Not everyone will inherit the Kingdom of God. There are multiple lists by Paul, Peter, John, James, and Jude that describe those continuing to live in sin as not inheriting the Kingdom of God. This cheap grace that covers your continual sin is not Biblical, according to the Apostles.

We Have Been Transferred to the Kingdom!

*He has delivered us from the domain of darkness and **transferred us to the Kingdom of the Son of God's love**.* (Colossians 1:13)

We are there now! He has delivered us and transferred us to the Kingdom!

God Calls You Into His Kingdom!

*For you know how, like a father with his children, we exhorted each one of you and encouraged you and charged you to walk in a manner worthy of **God, who calls you into His own Kingdom and glory**.* (1 Thessalonians 2:11-12)

Your mother or father or spouse or friend cannot call you into the Kingdom, but only God can, and He calls you into His glory also.

We are Heirs of the Kingdom, and It is a Promise!

*Listen, my beloved brothers and sisters, has not God **chosen** those who are poor in the world to be rich in faith and **heirs of the Kingdom, which He has promised** to those who love Him?* (James 2:5)

Our God Shall Reign Forever!

*Then the seventh angel blew his trumpet, and there were loud voices in heaven, saying, "The kingdom of the world has become **the Kingdom of our Lord and of His Christ, and He shall reign forever and ever.**"* (Revelation 11:15)

This Kingdom of God will last forever!

Jesus is King of the Kingdom!

And He has on His robe and on His thigh a name written: KING OF KINGS AND LORD OF LORDS. (Revelation 19:16)

Hear, O Israel, the Lord Your God is One!

And the LORD shall be King over all the earth. In that day it shall be—" The LORD is One," And His name One. (Zechariah 14:9-11)

Paul declared to the Elders of Ephesus that he was innocent of their blood because he taught them the Kingdom of God and that it was the will of God.

*Now I know that none of you among whom I have gone about **preaching the Kingdom** will ever see me again. Therefore, I declare to you today that **I am innocent of***

***the blood of any of you**. For I have not hesitated **to proclaim to you the whole will of God**.* (Acts 20:26)

The Gospel of the Kingdom of God is the whole will of God.

Philip preached the Gospel of the Kingdom of God:

*But when they believed Philip as he **proclaimed the Gospel of the Kingdom of God** and the name of Jesus Christ, they were baptized, both men and women.* (Acts 8:12)

Philip is called the Evangelist in Acts 21. An evangelist announces the coming of the King and his army. He preached the Gospel of the Kingdom of God, did signs and wonders, and baptized in the Name of Jesus. (...*they had only been baptized in the Name of the Lord Jesus.* Acts 8:16b)

The Good News of the Kingdom of God is that God now dwells in those who believe and obey Him. The King's domain is within us, His Body, and the King's dominion is over our lives. God has restored that which was lost- our walk with Him!

We can see from scripture that Jesus came to proclaim the Kingdom of God, which is here, now, at hand, within, and yet. This is the Gospel that Jesus taught, the Gospel of the Kingdom of God. Jesus taught His disciples to preach the Kingdom of God, and scripture confirms that the Gospel is the Kingdom of God through the book of Acts and the teachings of Paul. Paul actually tells the elders at Ephesus, when he was charging them with the teaching of **sound doctrine**, that he had taught them the **Kingdom of God**. He taught them how to enter the Kingdom of God, also. We will examine the Way that Jesus taught, but first, why do we have to do something to enter the Kingdom of God? God is holy, and we must be holy to be in the Kingdom. Our sin makes us unfit to be in the Kingdom of God, so God sent His only begotten Son, which is God with us, manifest in the flesh, to be our sacrifice for sin.

Sin and Righteousness

For all have sinned and fall short of the glory of God. (Romans 3:23)

We are sinners who miss the mark of where God wants us to be until we turn to Him (repent), get washed by the water for the forgiveness of sins (baptized, Acts 2:38), and get filled with His Holy Spirit, entering into the Kingdom of God, which is righteousness, peace and joy in the Holy Spirit.

Paul, Peter, James, Jude, and John gives lists of sin that will not inherit the Kingdom of God. We must be holy as He is holy (Leviticus 11:44-45; 1 Peter 1:15-16).

The Holy Spirit convicts us of our righteousness:

Nevertheless I tell you the truth. It is to your advantage that I go away; for if I do not go away, the Helper will not come to you; but if I depart, I will send Him to you. And when He has come, He will convict the world of sin, and of righteousness, and of judgment: of sin, because they do not believe in Me; ***of righteousness, because I go to My Father and you see Me no more;*** *of judgment, because the ruler of this world is judged* (John 16:7-11).

The Holy Spirit convicts the world of sin because they do not believe in Jesus, **convicts the believer of righteousness**, and Satan is judged. The word *convict* means to *convince* or to *shine light upon*. The Holy Spirit convicts and convinces believers of their righteousness! He has made us righteous and instruments of righteousness!

† Salvation and the Sound Doctrine of Paul

Soteriology is the study of salvation and how one becomes saved. The scriptures are clear on this, but doctrines of men and doctrines of unauthorized teachers have crept into the church, mainly influenced by pagan philosophy, pride, greed, Greek philosophy, and modern philosophy. There is a plan of salvation, called The Way, that Jesus laid out for us and taught His disciples to teach us. This is apostolic doctrine, teaching from the Lord and to His apostles to the church.

The Plan of Salvation is laid out in Acts 2:38, where the people are asking what they must do to be saved. This is the beginning of the Church and all throughout Acts this is how believers are added to the Church. Peter answers them:

Repent, and be baptized everyone of you in the Name of Jesus Christ for the forgiveness of sins, and you shall receive the gift of the Holy Spirit.

All of the apostles and the 120 were standing by him when he declared this and not one countered or corrected him, because he was teaching what Jesus had taught them and reiterated in the forty days He spent with them after His resurrection. Jesus had recently given Peter **the keys of the Kingdom** of God, and this is what Peter taught and commanded.

What Paul Declared to the Ephesian Elders in Acts 20:

- 21 *I have declared to both Jews and Greeks that they must turn to God in **repentance** and have faith in our Lord Jesus.*

- 24b *...my only aim is to finish the race and complete the task the Lord Jesus has given me—the task of testifying to the **Gospel of God's grace**.*

- 25b *...you among whom I have gone about **preaching the Kingdom***

- 27 *...For I have not hesitated to proclaim to you the **whole will of God**.*

Therefore: **Whole Will of God=Kingdom of God**

The Church is the Manifold Wisdom of God:

So that through the church the manifold wisdom of God might now be made known to the rulers and authorities in the heavenly places. This was according to the eternal purpose that He has realized in Christ Jesus our Lord (Ephesians 3:10-11).

The greatest creation of God is the Church, it is His manifold wisdom. All of the angelic beings stare down upon us in awe at what God has done.

The Kingdom of God is the King's Dominion and the King's Domain.

- His Domain and Dominion in Your Life
- His Domain and Dominion in His Body, the Church
- Righteousness, Peace, and Joy in the Holy Spirit
- Gifts of the Spirit
- Fruit of the Spirit
- Power in the Kingdom
- Entrance into the Kingdom
- We are Ambassadors of His Kingdom!

Peter was Given the Keys to the Kingdom:

<u>**The Keys to the Kingdom in Acts 2:38**</u>

- Repent
- Be Baptized Everyone of You in the Name of Jesus for the Forgiveness of Sins
- You Shall Be Filled with the Gift of the Holy Spirit (His Kingdom)

Paul Taught Acts 2:38 to the Ephesians!

Paul taught repentance to the Ephesians as sound doctrine:

*I have declared to both Jews and Greeks that they must turn to God in **repentance** and have faith in our Lord Jesus.* (Acts 20:21)

Paul Taught Water Baptism in the Name of Jesus as sound doctrine to the Ephesians:

*On hearing this, they were **baptized in the name of the Lord Jesus**.* (Acts 19:5)

Paul Taught the Infilling of the Holy Spirit as sound doctrine to the Ephesians:

*When Paul placed his hands on them, the **Holy Spirit came on them, and they spoke in tongues and prophesied**.* (Acts 19:6)

Each of these is separate events: repentance happened, baptism in water happened, and the infilling of the Holy Spirit happened, all at separate times, just as happened in Samaria with Phillips ministry.

Jesus Taught Acts 2:38!

Jesus Taught Repentance

Jesus also taught repentance, baptism in His Name, and the infilling of His Holy Spirit as sound doctrine:

*Now after that John was put in prison, Jesus came into Galilee, preaching the **Gospel of the Kingdom of God**, And saying, The time is fulfilled, and the **Kingdom of God** is at hand: <u>**repent, and believe the Gospel**</u>.* (Mark 1:14-15)

Jesus says that we must repent and believe the Gospel of the Kingdom of God.

Jesus Taught Baptism in His Name

Jesus Told Ananias to Baptize Paul in His Name:

*Then the Lord said, "**I am Jesus**, whom you are persecuting..."6 So he, trembling and astonished, said, "Lord, what do You want me to do?" Then the Lord said to him, "Arise and go into the city, and **you will be told what you must do.**"...17 And Ananias...laying his hands on him he said, "Brother Saul, the Lord Jesus, who appeared to you on the road as you came, has sent me that you may receive your sight and be filled with the Holy Spirit."* (Acts 9)

*16 And now what are you waiting for? Get up, be **baptized and wash your sins away, calling on the Name of the Lord.**'* (Acts 22)

Jesus instructed Ananias to baptize in His Name, instructing him to tell Paul that baptism in His Name would wash away Paul's sins. Therefore, Jesus instructed Ananias to baptize for the forgiveness of sins and to baptize specifically in the Name of Jesus, the only name that we can be saved by. Interesting to note here is that Paul asked God who He was, and He said 'I am

Jesus.' This explains why baptism was done in His Name, as we will examine later.

*Therefore go and make disciples of all nations, **baptizing them in the Name** of the Father and of the Son and of the Holy Spirit, and teaching them to obey everything I have commanded you. And surely I am with you always, to the very end of the age* (Matthew 28:19-20).

Jesus told the apostles to baptize in the **NAME** of the Father and of the Son and of the Holy Spirit. Every baptism done by the disciples in the book of Acts was done in the **Name of Jesus** and, according to Scripture, all of the Romans, Ephesians, Corinthians, Galatians, and Colossians were baptized in the Name of Jesus Christ. If all of the baptisms that occurred in the Book of Acts were done with the baptismal formula 'in the Name of Jesus', then I want to know why we baptize today mostly in the 'Name of the Father, and of the Son, and of the Holy Spirit', without actually invoking the Name of Jesus. Why and when did the baptismal formula change? What were the first century Jewish Christians doing and believing that convinced them to baptize in the name of Jesus?

Jesus Taught the Infilling of His Holy Spirit:

*Therefore go and make disciples of all nations, baptizing them in the Name of the Father and of the Son and of the Holy Spirit, and teaching them to obey everything I have commanded you. And surely **I am with you always**, to the very end of the age."* (Matthew 28:19-20)

Jesus is with us because His Holy Spirit dwells within believers hearts now!

I will not leave you as orphans; I will come to you (John 14:18).

Jesus, in describing the coming of the Holy Spirit upon believers, says that **He will come to us**. Paul says now the Spirit is the Spirit of the Lord, speaking of Jesus.

How to be Innocent of the Blood of the Unsaved

Paul told the elders at Ephesus that he was innocent of their blood because he had preached to them the Kingdom, which is the Gospel of the Kingdom of God. If we do not preach the Gospel of the Kingdom and the plan of salvation to enter the Kingdom, which is God's will, then we are guilty of the blood of those whom we have not shared the truth of Jesus to.

*Now I know that none of you among whom I have gone about **preaching the Kingdom** will ever see me again. Therefore, I declare to you today that I am **innocent of the blood of any of you**. For I have not hesitated to proclaim to you **the whole will of God**. Keep watch over yourselves and all the flock of which the Holy Spirit has made you overseers. Be shepherds of the **church of God, which He bought with His own blood**. I know that after I leave, savage wolves will come in among you and will not spare the flock. Even from your own number men will arise and **distort the truth** in order to draw away disciples after them. So be on your guard! Remember that for three years I never stopped warning each of you night and day with tears* (Acts 20:25-31).

Who is Paul saying will distort the truth?

Distort the Truth

- Savage Wolves
- Unauthorized Teachers
- False Teachers
- False Prophets
- False Apostles
- Wrongly Divided Word of God
- Less Accurate Teaching
- Pride, Unaccountable

Paul doesn't beat around the bush on this. He says that men from their own number, pastors and teachers and priests, will arise and distort the truth. Paul asked the Galatians who had bewitched them, who had lied to them and cast a spell on them by teaching them inaccurate doctrine. Paul writes to the Corinthians and asks them why they are continuing to sin and continuing to allow sinners to remain in the Church. Paul writes lists of sins that will not inherit the Kingdom of God. Peter writes lists of those who are sinning that will not be saved. Jude writes lists of sins that cannot be of God. In 177 AD the Montanists were excommunicated from the Roman church because they believed that prophecy was still a gift of the Holy Spirit, and they worshiped in the Spirit. In 325 AD Constantine completely took away the Hebrew aspect of the church, made it a state religion, and paved the way for the changing of the baptismal formula.

*So be on your guard! Remember that for three years I never stopped **warning each of you night and day with tears*** (Acts 20:31).

Warning and Tears Over Distorting the Truth!

Paul was warning against distorting the truth by distorting the Gospel of the Kingdom of God and who Jesus is and the Way of Salvation!

*"You are My witnesses," declares the LORD, "and My servant whom I have chosen, so that you may know and believe Me and understand that I am He. **Before me no god was formed, nor will there be one after Me**."* (Isaiah 43:10)

*I told you that you would die in your sins; **if you do not believe that I AM HE, you will indeed die in your sins**.* (John 8:24)

What is Truth?

- Jesus is our only God and Savior!
- We must repent!
- We must be baptized in the Name of Jesus!
- We will be filled with His Holy Spirit!
- This is the Kingdom of God and Jesus is King!

And without controversy great is the mystery of godliness: **God was manifest in the flesh** (1 Timothy 3:16)

Now to each one the **manifestation of the Spirit** *is given for the common good.* (1 Corinthians 12:7)

And I will pour out on the house of David and the inhabitants of Jerusalem a spirit of grace and supplication. **They will look on Me, the One they have pierced**, *and they will mourn for Him as one mourns for an only child, and grieve bitterly for Him as one grieves for a firstborn son.* (Zechariah 12:10)

God manifested Himself in the flesh as Jesus (Yahweh Salvation: I AM SALVATION), who is Emmanuel (God with US). God now manifests Himself as His Spirit into us, His Body, the Church.

✝ Foundational Principle Doctrines of Christ

*Therefore leaving the principles of the **doctrine of Christ**, let us go on unto perfection; not laying again the foundation of repentance from dead works, and of faith toward God, of the doctrine of baptisms, and of laying on of hands, and of resurrection of the dead, and of eternal judgment. (Hebrews 6:1-2)*

These are the six principle doctrines of Christ that Paul is telling us in Hebrews and also saying that we need to even get deeper in the Word and move forward in Christ. Many false or unauthorized teachers claim that these are law or legalism and that we are to move on from them. No, these are principle teachings of Christ. These principle doctrines of Christ are: Repentance; Faith; Baptisms; Laying On of Hands; Resurrection; and Eternal Judgment.

✝ Repentance

Jesus started and continued in His ministry preaching and proclaiming 'Repent! The Kingdom of God is at hand!' He taught that the Kingdom of God is at hand, here, now, within, and yet. You have to repent for the Spirit of God to dwell within you. The word 'repent' is from the Greek *metanoia*, meaning to change one's heart or mind. The English word 'repent' is from 're', to do again, like repeat, and 'pent' meaning uppermost place, like penthouse. We are to go again to the uppermost place where we walk with God! The only way this can happen is if we turn to God, which causes us to turn away from sin, because God is Holy. We cannot approach God with sin in our life or living in sin, which is why Paul writes six lists of sinful living that will not inherit the Kingdom of God and Peter writes three lists and John writes that we cannot continue in sin.

Hebrews calls this 'repentance from acts that lead to death.' This is sin in this life that leads to death, such as sexual sin can lead to diseases and cancer that can cause death, and continued sin that leads to eternal spiritual death.

† Faith Towards God

Faith towards God is belief and full commitment and covenant to Jesus Christ. Belief in Jesus is required for salvation, for there is no other Name that we can be saved by. God is One. The words 'belief' and 'faith' come from the Greek 'pistis,' meaning complete commitment and covenant with. The primary Greek word for "faith" in the Bible is pistis (πίστις), which signifies more than just intellectual belief, but encompassing trust, reliance, conviction, faithfulness, and a personal commitment or fidelity to God and His promises, often expressed through action, derived from the verb pisteuō (to believe/trust).

Our object of faith is Jesus Christ. We must love the Lord our God with all of our heart and soul. This is faith in our great God and Savior, Jesus Christ (Titus 2:13).

*For God so loved the world that He gave His only begotten **Son, that whosoever believes in Him** shall not perish but have eternal life.* (John 3:16)

On the day of Pentecost, the five thousand Jews had to repent and believe in Jesus and be baptized in the name of Jesus. They asked what they must do to be saved, and Peter told them to repent and be baptized, every one of you in the name of Jesus for the forgiveness of sins, and you shall be filled with the gift of the Holy Spirit. They all believed in the God of the Old Testament of their own imagination, but belief in Jesus was required for them to be saved, as it is for all mankind for the last two thousand years. You cannot be saved by believing the Trinity, or manifestations, or in God, or in gods- only by belief in Jesus. You can only be saved by the only Name that can save, the Name that is above all names, all names in heaven and in earth and below the earth, and this Name is Jesus. The Jews, the Samaritans, the Romans, the jailor, the Gentiles- all had to believe in Jesus to be saved. Jesus is how God has chosen to reveal Himself to us.

Our focus in belief is in Jesus. God has revealed Himself to us in the flesh (Emmanuel, God with us) and His highest revelation of His Name is Jesus. There are not two or three gods, there is only one God.

Hear O Israel, the Lord your God is One.

† Baptisms

Baptisms is plural in Hebrews 6 because there is baptism in water in the Name of Jesus for the forgiveness of sins and baptism in the Holy Spirit. These are two separate events in each of the occasions in the book of Acts.

In Acts 2 we see the 120 in the Upper Room filled with the Holy Spirit and speaking in tongues on the day of

Pentecost. They had already been baptized in Jesus' Name because they were disciples of Jesus (baptized in the Name of their Rabbi) and the disciples of John told John that Jesus was baptizing more than he was on the other side of the Jordan (although Jesus wasn't baptizing but his disciples were baptizing others in His Name) and the Pharisees said that Jesus was baptizing more disciples than John was. This is two separate events: the 120 disciples baptized and then later, after been told to tarry, filled with the Holy Spirit and speaking in tongues.

We see in Acts when Phillip goes to Samaria and people believe in Jesus after seeing the signs and wonders by Phillip that they are baptized in the Name of the Lord. The church sends out Peter and John from Jerusalem and they notice that none of them are filled with the Holy Spirit. They pray for them to receive the Holy Spirit and lay hands on them and they receive the Holy Spirit, which can be seen by others because Simon the Sorcerer wants to have this power. This is two separate events: Phillip baptizes the believers in Jesus' Name and later, after Peter and John pray for them and lay hands on them, they are filled with the Holy Spirit. We know they were baptized in water because Phillip baptized the Eunuch later in water.

Later in Acts, Peter is sent to the house of the Roman Cornelius by the Holy Spirit. As he is proclaiming the Word of the Lord to them the Holy Spirit falls on them and they speak with tongues and magnify God. Peter then asks if anyone can forbid them water and **commands** them to be baptized in the Name of Jesus.

This is two separate events: the believers in Cornelius' household were filled with the Holy Spirit and spoke in tongues and magnified God and then were commanded afterward to be baptized in the Name of Jesus.

In Acts 19 Paul comes across some disciples in Ephesus who have not heard of the Holy Spirit since they have believed. He then finds out they were baptized in the name of John and **immediately REBAPTIZES** (all baptisms in the New Testament were done immediately there was no waiting) them in the Name of Jesus and then lays hands on them and they are filled with the Holy Spirit and speak in tongues and prophesy. This is two separate events: the disciples are rebaptized in the Name of Jesus and then Paul lays hands on them and they are filled with the Holy Spirit and speak in tongues and prophesy.

All occasions of baptism in the book of Acts is done in the Name of Jesus as the baptismal formula. We have no other instances of any other name invoked in a baptism in the Church in the scriptures.

The arguments against baptism, saying that baptism is not necessary for salvation is a recent position brought about by unauthorized and false teachers. For almost two thousand years the church as a whole has believed that baptism in required for salvation and was first rejected by the Quakers and Salvation Army, and then by Calvinists. This is completely against scripture and Church history.

Jesus Himself said that 'those who believe and are baptized shall be saved' (Mark 16). Many churches reject the later part of Mark 16, mainly because of this scripture and the following scriptures defining the signs of believers casting out demons, speaking in tongues, and healing the sick. These are spiritually dead churches that argue against this. Their argument is from a textual position, arguing that the Majority Text doesn't include the latter portion of Mark 16. In reality there are 1853 ancient manuscripts that include the latter verses of Mark 16 and only two ancient texts that exclude it.

But Jesus isn't the only one who said that baptism is necessary for salvation: all of His apostles agreed that baptism was necessary. On the day of Pentecost, after Peter was given the keys of the Kingdom of God, and he stood up and preached Jesus Christ crucified and resurrected, they all asked what they should do to be saved. Peter replied: Repent, and be baptized every one of you in the Name of Jesus Christ for the forgiveness of sins, and you shall be filled with the gift of the Holy Spirit. Not one of the apostles or 120 disciples that were there countered him or corrected him. They all agreed that this is what the Lord had taught them. Peter, John, Phillip, and Paul commanded that the followers be baptized in Jesus Name in each baptism that occurred in the book of Acts. This is the apostles' doctrine that the church continued in.

In Acts 8:29-38, Phillip stops the chariot of the Ethiopian eunuch. If the eunuch only needed to believe, why stop the chariot? He already believed in God. If the eunuch only needed to pray a prayer, why stop the chariot (Mark 16:15-16)? If the eunuch only needed faith, why stop the chariot (James 2:24)? If baptism is not essential for salvation, why stop the chariot?

Every New Testament church was formed by those who were baptized after believing and repenting (Galatians 3:27; 1 Corinthians 12:13)

1. Church at Jerusalem, 3000 were baptized (Acts 2:41).
2. Church at Samaria, believed and were baptized, both men and women (Acts 8:12-16).
3. Church at Caesarea, Peter commanded them to be baptized (Acts 10:48).
4. Church at Philippi, Lydia and the Philippian jailer baptized (Acts 16:14-33).
5. Church at Corinth, believed and were baptized (Acts 18:8)
6. Church at Ephesus, Paul rebaptized disciples in the Name of Jesus (Acts 19:1-6).
7. Church at Galatia, believed Paul and baptized into Christ (Galatians 3:27).
8. Church at Colossae, were buried with Christ in baptism (Colossians 2:12).
9. Church at Rome, died to sin, then buried in baptism in Jesus Christ (Romans 6:1-4)
10. Church at Corinth, baptized in the Name of Jesus (1 Corinthians 1:13-15)

Many denominations and churches that do baptisms baptize in the name of the Father and of the Son and of the Holy Spirit. This baptismal formula is incorrect according to the scriptures and the teaching of Jesus and His apostles. This baptismal formula was added over four hundred years after Jesus by a church that was led by a state government led by Constantine.

Jesus did say to make disciples by baptizing them in the name of the Father and of the Son and of the Holy Spirit, but the verse before that says that the eleven worshiped Him. The only one that a Jew could worship was God. Not a man. Not another god. Only God. The women had already worshipped Him, which they could only worship God also. Following His command to them to make disciples by baptizing in the name of the Father and of the Son and of the Holy Spirit, **ALL apostles and ALL baptisms done in the book of Acts and mentioned in the other epistles are done in the NAME OF JESUS or the NAME OF THE LORD.** There is no other example of baptism in any other name in the scriptural church. This continued for hundreds of years in the historical early church.

There are only Biblical Reasons for Baptism in the Name of Jesus.

The Apostolic Church Adhered Exclusively to Baptism in the Name of Jesus

The Bible records five accounts of baptism in the New Testament church that describe a name or formula. Each case features the Name of Jesus.

The Jews in Jerusalem were baptized in the Name of Jesus:

*Peter replied, "Repent and **be baptized, every one of you, in the Name of Jesus Christ** for the forgiveness of* *your sins. And you will receive the gift of the Holy Spirit.* (Acts 2:38)

The believers in Samaria were baptized in the Name of Jesus:

When the apostles in Jerusalem heard that Samaria had accepted the word of God, they sent Peter and John to Samaria. When they arrived, they prayed for the new believers there that they might receive the Holy Spirit, because the Holy Spirit had not yet come on any of them; **they had simply been baptized in the Name of the Lord Jesus***. Then Peter and John placed their hands on them, and they received the Holy Spirit.* (Acts 8:14-17)

Acts 8 is critical in understanding repentance, baptism, and the infilling of the Holy Spirit. Here we see the believers in Samaria believe and accept the word of God, get baptized in the Name of Jesus, but not filled with the Holy Spirit until Peter and John lay their hands on them, showing that the infilling of the Holy Spirit is a separate event from either belief, repentance, and baptism.

The believers at Cornelius' house in Caesarea were baptized in water in the Name of Jesus:

Then Peter said, "Surely no one can stand in the way of their being baptized with water. They have received the Holy Spirit just as we have." **So he commanded that they be baptized in the name of Jesus Christ***. Then they asked Peter to stay with them for a few days.* (Acts 10:47-48)

The believers in Ephesus had been wrongly baptized and then **rebaptized** by **Paul in the Name of Jesus**:

Paul said, "John's baptism was a baptism of repentance. He told the people to believe in the one coming after him, that is, in Jesus." On hearing this, ***they were baptized in the name of the Lord Jesus****. When Paul placed his hands on them, the Holy Spirit came on them, and they spoke in tongues and prophesied.* (Acts 19:4-6)

Jesus instructed Ananias to baptize Paul in His Name. Note also that this baptism washes away sins:

And now what are you waiting for? ***Get up, be baptized and wash your sins away, calling on His Name.'*** (Acts 22:16)

'To call upon the Name of the Lord' means to be baptized into the name of the deity that you are invoking, which, in the Christian case, is the Name of Jesus.

The Epistles Refer Exclusively to Baptism in the Name of Jesus as the Baptismal Formula

The Romans were baptized into Christ Jesus:

Or don't you know that all of us who were ***baptized into Christ Jesus*** *were baptized into His death? We were therefore buried with Him through baptism into death in order that, just as Christ was raised from the dead through the glory of the Father, we too may live a new life.* (Romans 6:3-4)

The Corinthians were baptized in Jesus' Name:

*Is **Christ** divided? Was Paul crucified for you? Were you **baptized in the name** of Paul?* (1 Corinthians 1:13)

Paul, speaking to division in the Church of people following leaders such as Apollos, Peter, and Paul, asks if Christ is divided and if they were baptized in Paul's name, knowing that they were baptized in the Name of Jesus.

*And that is what some of you were. But **you were washed,** you were sanctified, you were justified **in the Name of the Lord Jesus Christ** and by the Spirit of our God.* (1 Corinthians 6:11)

The Galatians were baptized into the Name of Christ:

*For **all of you who were baptized into Christ** have clothed yourselves with Christ.* (Galatians 3:27)

The Colossians were baptized in the Name of Christ:

*For in Christ all the fullness of the Deity lives in bodily form, and in Christ you have been brought to fullness. He is the head over every power and authority. In Him you were also circumcised with a circumcision not performed by human hands. Your whole self ruled by the flesh was put off when **you were circumcised by Christ, having been buried with Him in baptism**, in which you were also raised with him through your faith in the working of God, who raised him from the dead.* (Colossians 2:9-12)

James tells his readers not to blaspheme the Name of Jesus which was called over them at baptism:

*Do they not blaspheme that **worthy Name that was called over you** at your baptism*? (James 2:7) (*Epikaleo* means to invoke, call upon, at the time of baptism)

Using the Name of Jesus in the Biblical baptismal formula expresses faith in:

1. The person of Christ (who He really is)
2. The work of Christ (death, burial, and resurrection for our salvation) and
3. The power and authority of Christ (ability to save us by Himself)

It is **a principle**- saving faith in the only Name where we can be saved. It is **a commandment** to be baptized in His Name according to Acts 2:38 and Acts 10:48. It is **a requirement** that must be fulfilled according to Mark 16:16 and John 3:5. Faith and baptism in the Name of Jesus is obedience that saves, and water baptism is not a work of man, but the work of God.

We do not have any scriptural evidence of baptisms done in the name of the Father and of the Son and of the Holy Spirit, only using the baptismal formula In the Name of Jesus. Historically, we see baptism following the Classical Trinitarian formula only 400 years later, and continuing to today. This is well after the bishop of Rome excommunicated the Phrygian church called the Montanists because they still spoke in tongues and worshipped in the Spirit and believed that the gift of prophecy and the spiritual gifts were still for today.

Call upon the Name

Some denominations and movements teach that all one has to do is call upon the Name of the Lord and they will be saved, thinking this phrase means to call upon Jesus. The phrase actually means 'to invoke the name of a deity at the time of baptism.' In our case, this would be to invoke the Name of Jesus at the time of baptism, which explains why all of the baptisms recorded in the book of Acts and all of the baptisms insinuated in the epistles where in the Name of Jesus. This is why, when Jesus sent Paul to Ananias on Straight Street and told Paul that Ananias would tell him everything he must do, that Ananias said to Paul, "**What are you waiting for, get up and be baptized, calling on the Name of the Lord**!" Jesus instructed Ananias to tell Paul to be baptized to wash away his sins and to call upon the Name of Jesus and that He wanted him to be filled with His Holy Spirit. Paul had already believed and repented when he met Jesus on the road to Damascus; he now needed to be baptized in the Name of Jesus and filled with the Holy Spirit.

This is also why the Scripture says to 'rightly divide the Word of God.' Some will claim that Romans 10 says you just call upon the name of the Lord and you will be saved. Well, we know that call upon the Name of Jesus means to call upon the Name of Jesus at the time of baptism. Who was the book of Romans written to, sinners or saints? It was not written to tell people how to get saved; only the book of Acts tell us this. It was written to the Church at Rome, which were all believers, and Romans 6 tells us that they were all already baptized into Christ and Romans 8 tells us that they were all already filled with the Holy Spirit.

This then brings us to Romans 10 again, where many argue that it says 'if you confess with your mouth and believe in your heart you will be saved' and that this means this is all one has to do to be saved. Paul is writing a letter to a church with already saved believers. They have repented, been baptized into Christ (chapter 6), and filled with the Holy Spirit (chapter 8). Their foundation to GET BAPTIZED IN THE NAME OF JESUS and TO BE FILLED WITH THE HOLY SPIRIT is to confess and believe. Confession of Jesus and belief in the resurrection are the two BASES of belief leading to obedience to Jesus Christ: repentance, baptisms, infilling of His Spirit.

In Acts, Paul and Silas are freed from jail by an earthquake. The jailer asked what he must do to be saved. Paul says to believe and you shall be saved, you and your household. Many theologians stop there and argue that all you have to do is believe, but the next verses have Paul explaining to the jailer and his household the Word of God and then baptizing him and his whole household. This is because belief is a full commitment and obedience to the Lord, including His baptism and infilling of His Spirit. This is why Paul in Acts 19 **REBAPTIZES** the Ephesian believers in the Name of Jesus and lays hands on them to be filled with the Holy Spirit, evidenced by them speaking in tongues and prophesying. If baptism and infilling of the Spirit didn't matter, Paul could have just let them go believing what they believed, but he corrected them and then brought them correctly into salvation and the Kingdom of God.

What Happens at Baptism?

According to the Word of God, not the false doctrine of men, at the time of baptism we are saved; our sins are forgiven and we are washed clean; our old sinful nature dies; we are buried with Christ; we are resurrected with Christ; we become a new creation with a new life; we are dead to sin; we have circumcision of the heart, both male and female; we put on Christ and the armor of light; and we are made a disciple of Christ.

Old Man Dies

What shall we say, then? Shall we go on sinning so that grace may increase? By no means! We are those who have died to sin; how can we live in it any longer? (Romans 6:1-2)

Paul writes to the Saints at Rome and tells them that they have died to sin and can therefore no longer wallow and live in it. How did we die to sin?

Or don't you know that all of us who were baptized into Christ Jesus were baptized into His death? (Romans 6:3)

Paul tells the saved Romans that we were all baptized in Christ Jesus (immersed in water as you will see) and at this moment in time we were baptized into His death.

New Creation Happens

Death to Sin

*We were therefore **buried with Him through baptism** into death in order that, just as Christ was raised from the dead through the glory of the Father, we too may live a new life* (Romans 8:4).

Paul tells the Romans (and by extension all obedient believers) that we were buried with Him through baptism. This burying happens when we are immersed in water and invoke the Name of Jesus.

We are Resurrected with Christ

***Baptism**, which corresponds to this, **now saves you** (not the removal of the filth of the flesh, but the pledge of a good conscience toward God) through the **resurrection of Jesus Christ**.* (1 Peter 3:21)

Forgiveness of Sins

*Peter replied: Repent, and be **baptized**, everyone of you, **for the forgiveness of sins**...*(Acts 2:38)

*And now what are you waiting for? Get up, **be baptized and wash your sins away, calling on the Name of the Lord.**'* (Acts 22:16)

Circumcision of the Heart

*In Him you were also circumcised with a circumcision not performed by human hands. Your whole self ruled by the flesh was put off when you were **circumcised by Christ, having been buried with Him in baptism**, in* *which you were also raised with Him through your faith in the working of God, who raised Him from the dead.* (Colossians 2:11-12)

Putting on Christ and the Armor of Light

*So in Christ Jesus you are all children of God through faith, for **all of you who were baptized into Christ have clothed yourselves with Christ**.* (Galatians 3:26-27)

The night is nearly over; the day is almost here. So let us put aside the deeds of darkness <u>and put on the armor of light</u>. Let us behave decently, as in the daytime, not in carousing and drunkenness, not in sexual immorality and debauchery, not in dissension and jealousy. Rather, <u>clothe yourselves with the Lord Jesus Christ</u>, and do not think about how to gratify the desires of the flesh. (Romans 12:12-14)

You are Made a Disciple of Christ

*Go into all the world and **make disciples, baptizing them**...*(Matthew 28)

No one is a disciple of Christ unless they have been baptized into His Name. I know this is hard to hear, but it is the Word of God. **We are to lead people to full obedience to God's plan for the New Testament Church.** No one has made any disciple of Jesus unless they have baptized them and commanded them to obey all that Jesus has taught (Matthew 28), which is written to us through the gospels, acts, and the epistles.

Salvation

***Baptism**, which corresponds to this, **now saves you** (not the removal of the filth of the flesh, but the pledge of a good conscience toward God) through the resurrection of Jesus Christ.* (1 Peter 3:21)

*Those who believe **and are baptized will be saved**...*(Mark 16:)

Baptism is not an outward expression of our faith, nor is it a public confession of our faith. Those are false doctrines of men. Baptism is obedience to Jesus Christ, leading to forgiveness of sins, eternal salvation, and entrance into the Church of God. We are to lead people to full obedience of God's plan for the New Testament Church.

We Have Personal Identification with Jesus Christ and His Name Identifies Us as His Possession

Baptism in the Name of Jesus scripturally is a personal identification with Jesus Christ, and His Name identifies us as His possession.

*Or don't you know that **all of us who were baptized into Christ Jesus were baptized into His death**?* (Romans 6:3)

Romans 6 states that all of the Roman believers were baptized in the Name of Jesus, and Paul clarifies that this baptism into Jesus identifies us with Christ and establishes that through this baptism a believer is united with Christ in His death and His resurrection. We have been buried with Christ in water and our old self and sin is dead, and the next verse establishes that we are resurrected with Christ and raised in baptism to walk in newness of life.

The whole assembly became silent as they listened to Barnabas and Paul telling about the signs and wonders God had done among the <u>Gentiles</u> through them. When they finished, James spoke up. "Brothers," he said, "listen to me. Simon has described to us how **God first intervened to choose a people for His Name from the Gentiles.** *The words of the prophets are in agreement with this, as it is written: "'After this I will return and rebuild David's fallen tent. Its ruins I will rebuild, and I will restore it, that the rest of mankind may seek the Lord, even all* **the Gentiles who bear My Name, says the Lord,** *who does these things'— things known from long ago.'" (Acts 15:12-17)*

In Acts 15, James, Peter, and Paul describe the Gentiles as becoming saved by taking on and bearing the Name of God, which we know they were all baptized into the Name of Jesus, which is the revealed Name of God to us that we bear His Name through baptism. What name did the Gentiles bear? It was the Name of Jesus! James in these verses is saying that Peter has said and both James and Paul agree, that this prophecy of God choosing His people from the Gentiles is fulfilled by them taking on His Name at baptism, which is the Name of Jesus, meaning that at this time the prophecy is fulfilled by baptism into His Name, which makes us His chosen bride.

James has interpreted through the Holy Spirit the meaning of Amos 9:11-12 as being fulfilled by the spreading of the Gospel of the Kingdom of God into the Gentile nations and the salvation of those **believers taking on and bearing the name of God, which is Jesus** in these verses.

*In that day "I will restore David's fallen shelter— I will repair its broken walls and restore its ruins— and will rebuild it as it used to be, so that they may possess the remnant of Edom and **all the Gentiles that bear My Name," declares the Lord**, who will do these things.* (Amos 9:11-12)

These three scriptures demonstrate that we are identified with Christ and take on and bear the Name of God when we are baptized in the Name of Jesus.

The Colossians were baptized in the Name of Jesus and identified with Him:

And having been buried with Him in baptism, you were raised with Him through your faith in the power of God, who raised Him from the dead. (Colossians 2:12)

The Galatians were baptized in the Name of Jesus and identified with Jesus:

For all of you who were baptized into Christ have clothed yourselves with Christ. (Galatians 3:27)

The Ephesians were baptized and buried with Christ and rose up in resurrection with Him and seated with Him in the Heavens:

...made us alive with Christ even when we were dead in our trespasses. It is by grace you have been saved! / And God raised us up with Christ and seated us with Him in the heavenly realms in Christ Jesus (Ephesians 2:5-6)

How were the Ephesians dead in their trespasses and then made alive? They were made alive by being baptized into Jesus. How were they raised up? Raised up with Jesus in baptism!

The Corinthians were buried with Christ in baptism and raised up a new creation identified with Christ:

Therefore if anyone is in Christ, he is a new creation. The old has passed away. Behold, the new has come! (2 Corinthians 5:17)

How did the Corinthians become 'in Christ'? Through baptism. How did they become a new creation? Through baptism. How did the old pass away? Through baptism.

Paul tells the Philippians that he is identified with Christ through baptism and therefore they are also:

I want to know Christ and the power of His resurrection and the fellowship of His sufferings, being conformed to Him in His death, / and so, somehow, to attain to the resurrection from the dead. (Philippians 3:10-11)

The name of Jesus represents all the power and authority of God. When we invoke His name in faith, His power and authority become available to us.

And Jesus came and spoke to them, saying, "All power is given unto me in heaven and in earth" (Matthew 28:18).

You may ask Me for anything in My Name, and I will do it, so that the Son may bring glory to the Father (John 14:14)

And when they had set them in the midst, they asked, "By what power, or by what name, have you done this?...Be it known unto you all, and to all the people of Israel, that by the name of Jesus Christ of Nazareth, whom you crucified, whom God raised from the dead, even by Him does this man stand here before you healed" (Acts 4:7,10).

Everything we do in word and deed should be done in the name of Jesus, and baptism is both word and deed.

And whatsoever you do in word or deed, do all in the Name of the Lord Jesus, giving thanks to God and the Father by Him (Colossians 3:17).

The name of the Lord Jesus Christ is the highest name known to humanity, and everyone will bow to that Name.

Wherefore God also has highly exalted Him, and given Him a Name which above every name; that at the Name of Jesus every knee shall bow, of things in heaven, and things in earth, and things under the earth; and that every tongue should confess that Jesus Christ is Lord, to the glory of God the Father (Philippians 2:9-10).

Baptism is part of our salvation (according to Jesus, Peter, and Paul), and Jesus is the only saving name.

*And everyone who calls on the **name of the Lord will be saved*** (Acts 2:21). (Peter is declaring that this outpouring of the Holy Spirit and baptism in the Name of Jesus is the fulfillment of the prophecy in Joel 2:32- *And everyone who **calls on the name of the Lord** will be saved*, and in Joel we know that this is God.)

*Salvation is found in no one else, for there is **no other name** under heaven given to mankind **by which we must be saved*** (Acts 4:12).

*Corresponding to that, **baptism now saves you**—not the removal of dirt from the flesh, but an appeal to God for a good conscience—**through the resurrection of Jesus Christ*** (1 Peter 3:21).

Baptism identifies us together with Christ and the Church and having faith in Jesus, signifying acceptance of Him as Savior, and Jesus is our only Savior and our only way to God.

*But when they believed Philip preaching the things concerning the Kingdom of God, and the name of Jesus Christ, **they were baptized**, both men and women* (Acts 8:12).

*And Philip said, "If you **believe** with all your heart, you may." And he answered and said, "I believe that Jesus Christ is the Son of God"* (Acts 8:37).

When they heard this, **they were baptized in the name of the Lord Jesus** *(Acts 19:5).*

Jesus answered, "I am the way and the truth and the life. No one comes to the Father except through me. If you really know me, you will know my Father as well. From now on, you do know him and have seen him." **Philip said, "Lord, show us the Father and that will be enough for us." Jesus answered: "Don't you know Me, Philip, even after I have been among you such a long time? Anyone who has seen Me has seen the Father.** *How can you say, 'Show us the Father'? Don't you believe that I am in the Father, and that the Father is in me? The words I say to you I do not speak on my own authority. Rather, it is the Father, living in Me, who is doing His work. Believe Me when I say that I am in the Father and the Father is in me; or at least believe on the evidence of the works themselves.* (John 14:6-11)

Baptism in Jesus' name signifies belief that the fullness of the Godhead (all divinity) is in Jesus, and we are complete in Him.

For in Him dwells all the fullness of the Godhead bodily, and you are complete in Him, which is the head of all principality and power (Colossians 2:9-10).

Baptism in the name of Jesus demonstrates reverence for and obedience to God's Word over human tradition.

Making the Word of God of no effect through your tradition, which you have delivered: and many such like things you do (Mark 7:13).

Beware lest any man spoil you through philosophy and vain deceit, after the tradition of men, after the rudiments of the world, and not after Christ (Colossians 2:8).

There is no performance or teaching in Scripture other than baptism in the Name of Jesus, so there is no theological justification for any other baptismal formula than in the Name of Jesus.

Hear, O Israel, the Lord your God is One (Deuteronomy 6:4).

For in Him dwells all the fullness of the Godhead bodily (Colossians 2:9).

Jesus tells the apostles to make disciples by baptizing them in the Name of the Father and of the Son and of the Holy Spirit. All of the baptisms done in the early church were done in the Name of Jesus, with the implication that we are *buried* with Jesus and *resurrected* with Him at this time. How can we be buried with the Father and Holy Spirit if they have not been buried and resurrected? The fullness of the Godhead was in Jesus! All that is God was in Jesus, the only Name by which we can be saved!

Therefore go and make disciples of all nations, baptizing them in the Name of the Father and of the Son and of the Holy Spirit, (Matthew 28:19)

This was the fulfillment of prophecy from the Lord in Ezekiel, that God would cleanse us and give us a new heart and a new spirit and that Spirit would be His Spirit that makes us righteous.

I will also sprinkle clean water on you, and you will be clean. I will cleanse you from all your impurities and all your idols. / I will give you a new heart and put a new spirit within you; I will remove your heart of stone and give you a heart of flesh. / And I will put My Spirit within you and cause you to walk in My statutes and to carefully observe My ordinances. (Ezekiel 36:25-27)

Christianity is monotheistic- there is only one God. Orthodox and Catholic and Reformed and Pentecostal Christianity teaches that there is only one God and that He came in the flesh in the Incarnation. There is no dualism, tritheism, polytheism, or denial of the deity of Jesus. There is only one God. We try to understand who God is by using terms such as trinity, triune, triunity, persons, persona, manifestations, etc., but there is only one God. The New Testament is First Century Jewish monotheism. They knew of only one God and they knew and spoke and wrote as Him coming and living with them and pouring out His Spirit on them, fulfilling all of prophecy. This One God asks us to believe in and take on the Name of Jesus.

Judas Did Not Believe that Jesus was God and Was Not Baptized

Judas addresses Jesus as "Rabbi" (meaning teacher) in Matthew 26:25 and Matthew 26:49. This is notable because the other disciples and apostles address Jesus as "Lord," as seen in Matthew 26:22, and the contrast in terminology highlights Judas's inability to see Jesus as God.

Then Judas, the one who would betray Him, asked, "Rabbi, am I the one?" (Matthew 26:25).

He went straight to Jesus, greeted Him, "How are you, Rabbi?" and kissed Him (Matthew 26:49).

In contrast, when the other disciples are asked about who will betray Jesus, they respond using "Lord." For example, in Matthew 26:22, one of the disciples asks, "*Is it I, Lord?*"

All of the Apostles read the Greek translation of the Old Testament known as the Greek Septuagint and knew that the word 'Lord' was the Greek '*Kyrios*', the word 'Lord' that was used in place of the Name of God which scholars think may be 'YAHWEH.' The disciples knew that He was God, but Judas did not; only simply as a teacher (Rabbi).

There is scholarly understanding that Judas was not baptized by Jesus as the other disciples had been.

Jesus answered, "Those who have been washed clean need only to wash their feet; their whole body is clean. And you are washed, though not every one of you." For He knew who was going to betray Him, and that was why He said not every one was washed clean (John 13:10-11).

Peter, Ananias, and Paul referred to baptism as being washed clean, and we know that Jesus baptized His disciples, eventually more than John the Baptist was doing, which would have been in His Name. Judas was not washed clean, and only had his feet washed.

After this, Jesus and His disciples went out into the Judean countryside, where He spent some time with them, and baptized...They came to John and said to him, "Rabbi, that man who was with you on the other side of the Jordan- the one you testified about- look, He is baptizing, and everyone is going to Him (John 3:22-29)

Now Jesus learned that the Pharisees had heard that He was gaining and baptizing more disciples than John, although in fact it was not Jesus who baptized, but His disciples (John 4:1-2).

Jesus' disciples were being baptized in the Name of Jesus, which is why the 120 in the upper room on the day of Pentecost were already baptized in His Name and Peter commanded the crowd to be baptized in the same Name they were baptized in.

The Difference between Acts and the Epistles

The Church began in Acts, which is the only book of the New Testament that explains how to enter the New Covenant and be saved. The letters from Romans to Revelation are not giving instructions on how to get saved, they are letters written to believers who were already baptized in the name of Jesus, already born of the water and the Spirit, and already entered into the Kingdom of God. This is through the sound doctrine of belief, repentance, baptism, and the infilling of the Holy Spirit. The mention of baptism in these letters in not giving instructions to unbelievers on how to get saved. The books from Romans to Revelation are not explaining how to enter the covenant, but are teaching believers how to live in the Church. When baptism is mentioned in the epistles and other books after Acts, it is speaking of something that has already happened to the believers that are reading this epistle or book, reminding them of when they entered into Christ, explaining and not replacing the meaning and results of baptism, and calling the believers to live a sanctified life consistent with what baptism has accomplished through Christ.

In the epistles, Paul never describes baptism as symbolic, an outward side, optional, or future. He describes baptism as a completed act that has already placed baptized believers in Christ, in the body, under the new covenant, and in His death and resurrection. Paul always uses past tense language in his epistles, such as 'you were buried with Him,' 'you have put on Christ,' 'you were baptized.' Baptism in the epistles is a foundation already laid and a new life begun, not a suggestion waiting to be obeyed or not obeyed. Acts shows us how to be saved and enter the new covenant and the rest of the New Testament shows how we are to live a holy life in Him. The letters to the Church from Romans through Revelation are written to saved believers in the Church who have repented and been baptized into the name of Jesus, not to the world. The believers who are reading these letters are already described by the writers as sanctified, justified, washed, in Christ, in the body, and partakers of the Holy Spirit. These descriptions only apply to believers who have already obeyed the gospel and have been saved and brought into the Kingdom of God.

Baptism in the Holy Spirit

The second baptism is baptism in the Holy Spirit. Jesus told His disciples to go to Jerusalem and wait or tarry until they received power from on high. On the day of Pentecost, as the 120 disciples were praying, the Holy Spirit fell on them and they spoke in tongues and magnified God. The surrounding people thought they were drunk early in the morning because they could **SEE THAT THEY ACTED SOMEHOW DRUNK**. Peter then boldly witnessed to them and told them that what they are seeing is the fulfillment of the prophecy of Joel 2 and that they had crucified the Messiah, who is God over all. They then asked what they must do to be saved and Peter replied: Repent, and be baptized every one of you in the Name of Jesus Christ for the forgiveness of sins and you shall be filled with the gift of the Holy Spirit. Every occasion in the book of Acts where someone is filled with the gift of the Holy Spirit, they speak with tongues AND either prophesy or magnify God. This is the entrance into the Kingdom of God that Peter was given the keys to. God poured His Spirit out onto men and women and they speak with new tongues and prophesy. This is the Kingdom of God: righteousness, peace, and joy in the Holy Spirit.

For the Spirit of God to dwell in us, His Body, the Church, we must be holy, because He is a Holy God. God walked with us in the Garden of Eden, was in the cloud during the desert, was in the Tabernacle/Temple, walked with us on earth as Emmanuel (God with Us), then poured His Spirit out on us and dwells in His tabernacle, us, His church, now.

Power from On High

*Behold, **I send the Promise** of My Father upon you; but tarry in the city of Jerusalem until you are endued with **power from on high** (Luke 24:49).*

*On one occasion, while He was eating with them, He gave them this command: "Do not leave Jerusalem, but **wait for the gift** my Father promised, which you have heard Me speak about (Acts 1:4).*

The Holy Spirit came upon the church on the day of Pentecost in Acts 2. Jesus had told His disciples to tarry and He would send the Promise to them, which was power from on high. These disciples tarried and prayed for ten days for the Spirit to come upon them, as Jesus had instructed them. Jesus was resurrected on Easter and then for forty days He appears to His disciples teaching them about the Kingdom of God (Acts 1:3). On day 40 Jesus ascends into heaven (Acts 1:9). The disciples then tarry in Jerusalem, praying and expecting the promised gift (Acts 1:4). On Pentecost, day 50, the Holy Spirit descends with a sound like a rushing wind and tongues of fire, empowering the disciples, marking the birth of the Church (Acts 2:1-4).

Each instance of the infilling of the Holy Spirit into believers in the book of Acts comes with speaking in tongues, prophesying, and/or magnifying God. Each instance of the infilling of the Holy Spirit is observable by those that are around them, as in the case on the day of Pentecost when they thought they were drunk, when Peter and John and Simon the sorcerer could see that they were filled with the Holy Spirit and Simon wanted to buy that ability, when Peter and those with him at Cornelius' house saw them speak with tongues and commanded them to be baptized in the name of Jesus, and when Paul laid his hands on the believers in Ephesus and he could see them filled with the Holy Spirit and speak with tongues. In each instance of the infilling of the Holy Spirit it is a separate event from belief, repentance, and water baptism in the name of Jesus.

He said to them, "Go into all the world and preach the gospel to all creation. Whoever believes and is baptized will be saved, but whoever does not believe will be condemned. And **these signs will accompany those who believe: In My Name** *they will drive out demons;* **they will speak in new tongues**... (Mark 16:15-17).

Jesus says that those who believe in Him will speak in tongues, along with other signs. A sign signifies that someone has been to a specific place. It is how one can track and see evidence that someone has been to a place. If a Christian who believes Jesus and believes that the Holy Spirit of God dwells in them has been to a place/area/region, one can tell by the signs, their signature, that they have been there by their gifts, which Jesus states here is individual deliverance, speaking in tongues, regional deliverance, not being poisoned and polluted by the world, and healing.

These are not the only gifts of the Holy Spirit, though. The New Testament identifies approximately 28 gifts of the Holy Spirit, along with the fruit of the Spirit. It is not the purpose of this book to describe how each of these gifts and fruit operate in the Body of Christ, His church, but to note that the infilling of the Holy Spirit is Sound Doctrine according to Paul's charge and the evidence of the Scriptures.

Part of the Good News of the Kingdom of God is that the gift of the Holy Spirit is a **Promise from God**!

*Peter replied, "Repent and be baptized, every one of you, in the name of Jesus Christ for the forgiveness of your sins. And **you will receive the gift of the Holy Spirit. The Promise is for you and your children and for all who are far off—for all whom the Lord our God will call*** (Acts 2:38-39).

The Promise of the Holy Spirit is not only for us but for our children and our descendants also!

Partial List of Gifts of the Holy Spirt:

A list of some of the gifts of the Holy Spirit as they appear in the New Testament includes: Apostles; Prophets; Pastor; Teachers; Evangelists; Prophecy; Teaching; Word of Wisdom; Word of Knowledge; Faith; Miraculous Powers (Operations); Healings; Discernment of Spirits; Speaking in Tongues; Interpretation of Tongues; Helps (Deacons); Service; Administrations (Governments); Encouragement; Counseling; Giving; Leadership; and Mercy.

Note that some of these gifts are people, such as prophet, pastor, teacher, operations, and deacons. The gift is in you and you with the Spirit are the gift to the church.

*But grace was given to each one of us according to the measure of Christ's gift. Therefore it says, "When He ascended on high He led a host of captives, and **He gave gifts to men."**... And He gave **apostles, prophets, evangelists, pastors, and teachers**, to equip the saints for the work of ministry, for the edification of the body of Christ* (Ephesians 4:7-8, 11-12).

*And **God** has appointed (Greek tithemi: set, ordained, established) these in the church: first **apostles**, second **prophets**, third **teachers**, after that **miracles**, then **gifts of healings, helps, administrations, varieties of tongues*** (1 Corinthians 12:28).

These are all people that are the gifts!

Note also that some of these gifts are for the edification of the individual believer and some are for the edification of the church.

*And He gave **apostles, prophets, evangelists, pastors, and teachers**, to equip the saints for the work of ministry, **for the edification of the body of Christ*** (Ephesians 4:11-12).

*Anyone who **speaks in a tongue edifies themselves**, but the **one who prophesies edifies the church*** (1 Corinthians 14:4).

Speaking in tongues (glossolalia) primarily builds up or strengthens the individual speaker spiritually, like building a house (edifice) for God's revelation, while prophecy builds up the church; however, tongues can edify the church if interpreted, as the goal of all spiritual gifts is the common good and growth of the entire

Christian body. It's seen as a private prayer language for personal spiritual recharging, but needs interpretation for public teaching.

Self-Edification: Speaking in tongues is described as strengthening one's own faith and spirit, a private conversation with God that builds up the believer internally, often described as "praying in the Holy Spirit."

Church Edification (with interpretation): For the church to benefit, the message spoken in tongues must be interpreted into a known language, allowing the congregation or individual to receive encouragement, instruction, and growth, similar to prophecy.

Balance: The Apostle Paul emphasized that while self-edification is valuable, prophecy (speaking a known message) is superior in public settings because it builds up the whole church, highlighting the need for balance between personal experience and communal benefit.

Now I wish that you would all speak in tongues, but even more that you would prophesy; and greater is one who prophesies than one who speaks in tongues, unless he interprets, so that **the church may receive edification** *(1 Corinthians 14:5).*

Note also that there is a ranking order in the church of some of these gifts that operate as functional roles of leadership in the church, as God has set in the church according to 1 Corinthians 12:28.

And **God** *has appointed (Greek tithemi: set, ordained, established) these in the church:* **first** *apostles,* **second** *prophets, **third** teachers, **after that** miracles, **then** gifts of healings, helps, administrations, varieties of tongues* (1 Corinthians 12:28).

This is a ranking order that the Holy Spirit of God has given Paul to write to the church at Corinth. First (proton), second (deuteron), third (triton) are a ranking order of how God established the church and wants operational ministry to occur. This is further discussed in my book *Operational Ministry: The Structure and Operations of the Church and Functional Roles of Church Officers*.

The purpose of these gifts of the Holy Spirit are that we (the Church, which is the manifest wisdom of God) are edified in order to attain to the UNITY of the faith and the knowledge of the Son of God.

*And He Himself gave some to be apostles, some prophets, some evangelists, and some pastors and teachers, for the equipping of the saints for the work of ministry, for the edifying of the body of Christ, till we all come to the **unity of the faith and of the knowledge of the Son of God**, to a perfect man, to the measure of the stature of the fullness of Christ; that we should no longer be children, tossed to and fro and carried about with every wind of doctrine, by the trickery of men, in the cunning craftiness of deceitful plotting* (Ephesians 4:11-14).

This 'unity' is the Greek *henotēs* (εἷς), meaning 'oneness' in Classical Greek. What is this 'oneness' about? Why is this 'oneness' so important? Jesus prayed that we, the church, would be one with Him and the Father.

This oneness or unity of the faith includes **the knowledge of the Son of God**:

*Until we all come to the **unity of the faith and of the knowledge of the Son of God**, to a perfect man, to the measure of the stature of the fullness of Christ* (Ephesians 4:13).

Why would Paul be telling the church at Ephesus that they needed to come to the knowledge of the Son of God? Wouldn't the Christian church at Ephesus know about Jesus? Haven't the apostles, prophets, and evangelists already told the believers about who Jesus is? Why would there need to be teachers and pastors to bring professing believers to the unity of the faith and the knowledge of the Son of God? What more knowledge about the Son of God do we need to know so much that when Jesus ascended on high He left gifts such as apostles, prophets, evangelists, pastors, and teachers that we need to all come to a more complete knowledge of Him? Is there doubt in some believers that Jesus is God? Of course there is, in that amongst the eleven apostles in Matthew 8, even though they worshiped Him, some had doubt:

*Then **the eleven disciples** went to Galilee, to the mountain where Jesus had told them to go. When they saw Him, **they worshiped Him**; **but some doubted*** (Matthew 28:16-17).

These are the apostles that spent three years with Jesus. One had already betrayed Him, one had not believed it was Him resurrected, one had denied Him, and some doubted that He was God, even though they worshiped Him. This is because we all need to come to an understanding of the **FULLNESS OF CHRIST**:

*Until we all come to the **unity of the faith and of the knowledge of the Son of God**, to a perfect man, to the measure of the stature of **the fullness of Christ*** (Ephesians 4:13)

In Jesus Christ dwells the fullness of the Godhead bodily, not the partialness. Jesus is the express image of God. There is no other way that we can see Him. God was IN Christ, reconciling the world to Himself. This is why Jesus said, 'If you have seen Me, you have seen the Father.' This is why He said, 'What do you mean show you the Father, haven't I been with you long enough.'

Jesus left us apostles, prophets, evangelists, pastors, and teachers so that we are not seduced by various false doctrines that are created by men, tradition, pride, or demons. This is the whole purpose and reason that Paul was charging church leaders with **SOUND DOCTRINE**.

*That we should no longer be children, tossed to and fro and **carried about with every wind of doctrine**, by the trickery of men, in the cunning craftiness of deceitful plotting* (Ephesians 4:14).

How much of the Godhead is in Christ Jesus? All of God!

*He who descended is also the One who ascended far above all the heavens, that **He might fill all things*** (Ephesians 4:10).

*One God and Father of all, who is over all and through **all and in all*** (Ephesians 4:6).

*And there are diversities of operations, but it is **the same God which works all in all**.* 1 Corinthians 12:6

*Here there is not Greek and Jew, circumcised and uncircumcised, barbarian, Scythian, slave, free; but **Christ is all, and in all*** (Colossians 3:11).

*That **God may be all in all*** (1 Corinthians 15:28).

There is only one God in Christianity, and He is all in all. Jesus is the image of the invisible God, Jesus created all things, and He is before all things, and in Him all things consist.

He is the image of the invisible God, *the firstborn over all creation. For by Him **all things were created that are in heaven and that are on earth**, visible and invisible, whether thrones or dominions or principalities or powers. **All things were created through Him and for Him. And He is before all things, and in Him all things consist*** (Colossians 1:15-17).

The Fruit of the Spirit

Belief, repentance, and baptism bring us the Promise of the Holy Spirit, and this baptism of the Holy Spirit brings us both gifts and fruit of the Spirit. If the gifts of the

Spirit are for equipping the Saints for the work of the ministry and edifying the Saints so that we come to the unity of the faith and knowledge of the Son of God, the fruit of the Spirit are the emanation of the Spirit of God dwelling in us to each other, the world, and to God Himself. Paul lists the fruit of the Spirit in Galatians 5:22-23, which lists them as love, joy, peace, forbearance (patience), kindness, goodness (generosity), faithfulness, gentleness, and self-control, stating that against such things there is no law. Other related verses, like John 15:5-8, emphasize the source of this fruit in Jesus (the vine) and the importance of bearing good fruit to know true believers.

But the fruit of the Spirit is love, joy, peace, patience, kindness, generosity, faithfulness, gentleness and self-control. Against such things there is no law (Galatians 5:22-23).

Although it is called the fruit of the Spirit, Jesus says the source of this fruit is Him:

I am the vine; you are the branches. If you remain in Me and I in you, you will bear much fruit; apart from Me you can do nothing (John 15:5-8).

Notice that we must **remain or abide in Him**.

*You will **recognize them by their fruits**. Do people pick grapes from thornbushes, or figs from thistles* (Matthew 7:16).

Jesus also says the importance of bearing good fruit is to know true believers and the world can recognize us also. Just like the gifts of the Spirit, the fruit is observable and recognizable. We are to have hope, joy, patience, and peace, and are commanded to love one another.

May the God of hope fill you with all joy and peace as you trust in him, so that you may overflow with hope by the power of the Holy Spirit (Romans 15:13).

Jesus says that He is the source of the fruit, but God is the God of hope that gives us joy and peace, but this comes from the power of His Holy Spirit. That can only occur if God is One, and He is.

Therefore, as God's chosen people, holy and dearly loved, clothe yourselves with compassion, kindness, humility, gentleness and patience. Bear with each other and forgive one another if any of you has a grievance against someone. Forgive as the Lord forgave you. And over all these virtues put on love, which binds them all together in perfect unity. Let the peace of Christ rule in your hearts, since as members of one body you were called to peace. And be thankful (Colossians 3:12-15).

Paul writes to the Colossians and encourages believers, as God's chosen people, to "put on" virtues like compassion, kindness, humility, gentleness, and patience, alongside forgiveness (as Christ forgave them) and love, which binds all things together, all while letting the peace of Christ rule in their hearts and being thankful. It's a call to live out their faith through specific character traits that reflect God's nature, fostering unity and peace within the Christian community.

The key virtues of Colossians 3 are (v. 12):

1. Compassionate hearts/Tender mercy: Deep empathy and care for others.
2. Kindness: Friendly, generous, and considerate behavior.
3. Humility: A modest view of one's own importance.
4. Gentleness/Meekness: Strength under control, being mild-mannered.
5. Patience/Longsuffering: Enduring hardship and provocation without complaint.

The interpersonal actions of Colossians 3 are (v. 13):

1. Bear with one another: Tolerate each other's faults.
2. Forgive one another: Let go of grievances, just as Christ forgave you.

The supreme virtue of the believer in Colossians 3 (v. 14);

1. Love: The most important quality, binding all the others in perfect harmony and unity.

The result of these virtues (v. 15):

1. Peace of Christ: Let Christ's peace govern your heart.
2. Thankfulness: Be grateful.

† Doctrine of Laying On of Hands

The Doctrine of the Laying On of Hands includes laying on of hands for healing, for impartation of gifts of the Spirit, for the infilling of the Holy Spirit, for ordination, and for sending.

James says, *'Is anyone among you sick? Let them call the elders of the church to pray over them and anoint them with oil in the name of the Lord.'* (James 5:14).

When we pray for someone and anoint them with oil we are laying hands on them in the name of Jesus for healing.

Peter and John lay hands on the believers in Samaria and they receive the Holy Spirit:

Then Peter and John laid their hands on them, and they received the Holy Spirit (Acts 8:17).

Paul lays hands on the disciples in Ephesus and they receive the Holy Spirit and speak in tongues and prophesy:

And when Paul had laid his hands upon them, the Holy Spirit came on them, and they spoke with tongues and prophesized (Acts 19:6).

Paul and Barnabus have hands laid on them and sent out to the gentiles to minister:

So after they had fasted and prayed, they laid their hands on them and sent them off (Acts 13:3).

Paul writes to the Romans that he longs to see them to impart into them a gift to strengthen them, linking the impartation of spiritual gifts to the laying on of hands:

I long to see you so that I may impart to you some spiritual gift to strengthen you (Romans 1:11).

Paul writes Timothy and tells him to stir up the gift that is in him by the laying on of hands, again linking the impartation of spiritual gifts to the laying on of hands:

Fan into flame the gift of God, which is in you through the laying on of my hands (2 Timothy 1:6).

† Doctrine of Resurrection of the Dead

At that moment the curtain of the temple was torn in two from top to bottom. The earth shook, the rocks split and the tombs broke open. The bodies of many holy people who had died were raised to life. They came out of the tombs after Jesus' resurrection and went into the holy city and appeared to many people. (Matthew 27:51-53)

These were not the patriarchs that were raised from the dead, but more than likely disciples of Jesus who had passed while he was teaching because they were holy saints that were raised to life. The tombs opened up at the crucifixion and AFTER Jesus' resurrection they were raised to life, Jesus still being the firstfruits of resurrection. Believers will be resurrected to dwell with God forever.

And if the Spirit of Him who raised Jesus from the dead is living in you, He who raised Christ from the dead will also give life to your mortal bodies because of His Spirit who lives in you (Romans 8:11).

Paul describes our resurrection occurring at the time of baptism in the name of Jesus:

We were therefore buried with Him through baptism into death in order that, just as Christ was raised from the dead through the glory of the Father, we too may live a new life. For if we have been united with Him in a death like His, we will certainly also be united with Him in a resurrection like His. (Romans 6:4-5).

Paul tells the Romans (and by extension all obedient believers) that we were buried with Him through baptism. This burying happens when we are immersed in water. This union with Him in baptism leads to resurrection with Him.

Jesus said to her, "I am the resurrection and the life. The one who believes in Me will live, even though they die; and whoever lives by believing in Me will never die. Do you believe this?" (John 11:25).

Jesus is the resurrection and this new and eternal life that we will live.

† Doctrine of Eternal Judgment

Biblical eternal judgment is the final, permanent divine sentence where God judges all people based on their deeds and faith in Jesus Christ, separating the righteous for eternal life and the wicked for everlasting punishment (hell/destruction) in events like the Sheep and Goats (Matthew 25) and Revelation, a definitive end with no appeals, establishing justice for all actions.

Jesus says that we will be judged by His Word.

The one who rejects me and does not receive My words has a judge; the word that I have spoken will judge him on the last day. (John 12:48)

Jesus will judge us by His Word. Not the word of man or doctrines of men, but by His Word. He says that 'If you do not believe I AM HE, you will die in your sins.'

The Key Aspects of Eternal Judgment are:

1. Universal and Impartial: Everyone who has ever lived will stand before God, judged by His perfect standards, not human ones, with no favoritism (Romans 2:11, 2 Corinthians 5:10).
2. Based on Deeds and Faith: Judgment considers actions, words, and the presence or absence of faith in Christ, separating believers from unbelievers (Matthew 25:31-46, John 6:29).
3. Finality: The sentences (eternal life or everlasting punishment/destruction) are final, with no second chances or appeals after death (Hebrews 9:27, Matthew 25:46).

4. Jesus as Judge: Jesus Christ, to whom all judgment has been given, will preside over this judgment (John 5:22, Matthew 25:31).
5. Consequences: The righteous enter eternal life; the unrighteous face "everlasting punishment" or "eternal destruction" in "everlasting fire," described as the lake of fire (Matthew 25:46, Revelation 20:10-15).

Some of the key Scriptural references for eternal judgement are:

1. Matthew 25:31-46: The separation of sheep (righteous) and goats (wicked).
2. John 5:22, 29: Jesus as judge, resurrection of life vs. resurrection of judgment.
3. Romans 2:5-11: God's judgment according to truth and deeds.
4. Hebrews 6:2: Lists eternal judgment as a foundational doctrine.
5. Revelation 20:11-15: The great white throne judgment and the lake of fire.

† The Resurrection Power of Jesus Christ through Baptism in Romans 6

1 What shall we say, then? Shall we go on sinning so that grace may increase? 2 By no means! We are those who have died to sin; how can we live in it any longer?

Paul writes to the Saints at Rome and tells them that they have died to sin and can therefore no longer wallow and live in it. How did we die to sin?

3 Or don't you know that all of us who were baptized into Christ Jesus were baptized into His death?

Paul tells the saved Romans that we were all baptized in Christ Jesus (immersed in water as you will see) and at this moment in time we were baptized into His death.

4 We were therefore buried with Him through baptism into death in order that, just as Christ was raised from the dead through the glory of the Father, we too may live a new life.

Paul tells the Romans (and by extension all obedient believers) that we were buried with Him through baptism. This burying happens when we are immersed in water.

5 For if we have been united with Him in a death like His, we will certainly also be united with Him in a resurrection like His.

When were we united with Him in a death like His? At baptism, when we are buried with Him! When are we united with Him in a resurrection? At baptism, when we come up out of the water! Paul does a play with the Greek word for united, *symphytos*. It literally means *'with plan't*, meaning we have been planted together, like a seed, and spring up together, with life.

6 For we know that our old self was crucified with Him so that the body ruled by sin might be done away with, that we should no longer be slaves to sin— because anyone who has died has been set free from sin.

When were we crucified with Him? Certainly none of us were hanging on the cross with Him. We were crucified with Him at baptism! That is when we died to sin- at baptism. Jesus hung on that cross and shed His blood to cover our sins, but in His infinite wisdom He has designed baptism in His Name to be the covenant for us to join Him.

8 Now if we died with Christ, we believe that we will also live with Him.

When did we die with Christ? At baptism! When did we rise with Him? At baptism! We will live with Him forever being baptized into Him!

9 For we know that since Christ was raised from the dead, He cannot die again; death no longer has mastery over Him. The death He died, He died to sin once for all; but the life He lives, He lives to God.

He died for our sins once, and asks us to be obedient to Him to enter into that cleansing forgiveness. Since we have entered into that death and resurrection with Him, we live for God now!

11 In the same way, count yourselves dead to sin but alive to God in Christ Jesus.

How are we dead to sin? Through baptism! How are we alive to God? Through baptism! God was in Christ Jesus reconciling the world to Himself.

12 Therefore do not let sin reign in your mortal body so that you obey its evil desires.

We are to sin no more and be holy, as He is holy. This is a real concept. The Old Testament points to Christ, but describes how to be holy. Paul, Peter, and John write epistles that have lists of sins that will not inherit the Kingdom of God.

13 Do not offer any part of yourself to sin as an instrument of wickedness, but rather offer yourselves to God as those who have been brought from death to life; and offer every part of yourself to Him as an instrument of righteousness.

We are God's instruments of righteousness in this world. Because He has chosen us and has chosen to dwell in us, we are to not sin. Peter writes that *'we are to confess our sins to one another that we might be healed.'* The same Greek word for healed in this verse also means saved. Jesus says that the Holy Spirit will convict us of our righteousness, meaning that sin has no place in our bodies and that we are to be righteous.

14 For sin shall no longer be your master, because you are not under the law, but under grace.

As we can see in the previous verses, this grace is not freedom to sin, but freedom from sin and the gift of righteousness that He has imputed to us.

The Scriptures Identify the Godhead as Raising Jesus

*But **God raised Him from the dead**, freeing Him from the agony of death, because it was impossible for death to keep its hold on Him. (Acts 2:24)*

***The Holy Spirit raised Jesus from the dead**. If the same Holy Spirit lives in you, He will give life to your bodies in the same way. (Romans 8:11)*

***Jesus** answered them, "Destroy this temple, and **I will raise it** again in three days"(John 2:19).*

As we can observe from the Scriptures, God resurrected Jesus, as did Holy Spirit, but Jesus said that He will raise Himself up. Who resurrected Jesus? Jesus did, as the fullness of the Godhead dwelled within Him.

This same Spirit of Resurrection lives within us now:

And if the Spirit of Him who raised Jesus from the dead is living in you, He who raised Christ from the dead will also give life to your mortal bodies because of His Spirit who lives in you (Romans 8:11).

Jesus said to her, "I am the resurrection and the life. The one who believes in Me will live, even though they die; and whoever lives by believing in Me will never die. Do you believe this?" (John 11:25).

† Jesus is God

God has revealed Himself to us in both general revelation and special revelation. General revelation is God's revelation to us through His creation, especially expressed to us in Romans 1:

The wrath of God is being revealed from heaven against all the godlessness and wickedness of people, who suppress the truth by their wickedness, since **what may be known about God is plain to them, because God has made it plain to them. For since the creation of the world God's invisible qualities—His eternal power and divine nature—have been clearly seen, being understood from what has been made, so that people are without excuse.** For although they knew God, they neither glorified him as God nor gave thanks to him, but their thinking became futile and their foolish hearts were darkened (Romans 1:18-21).

Theology is the study of God. Without faith it is impossible to please God, because you must first believe that He exists, and is a rewarder of those who seek Him diligently. Our goal should be to seek Him, study Him, and reflect upon Him and His Word.

Special revelation is through both His written word (logos) and spoken word (rhema). This revelation is given to us by the Holy Spirit Who convicts the world of sin by not believing on Jesus (God Who Saves).

Great are the works of the Lord, studied by all who delight in them. (Psalm 111:2)

Who is Jesus?

On the day of Pentecost the Holy Spirit came upon believers and Peter gave a sermon to all of the Jews listening in Jerusalem. The Jewish people were convicted in their hearts that they had crucified the Messiah, and asked what they must do to be saved. Peter replied with all the other apostles and disciples around him, that "they must repent, and be baptized every one of you in the name of Jesus Christ for the forgiveness of sins and you shall be filled with the gift of the Holy Spirit," explaining to them that was what they were observing on the believers when they saw them speaking in tongues and magnifying God. Those who accepted his message were baptized and three thousand were added to the church that day.

Those three thousand Jews the day before believed in God, but only a god of their own making and understanding. They had to believe in Jesus, the one true, living God, who had come in the flesh as their Messiah in order for them to be saved.

One cannot just believe in God and be saved, otherwise none of those Jews who thought they believed in the God of Israel would have to repent, be baptized into the name of Jesus Christ for the forgiveness of sins, and be filled with the Holy Spirit of God in order to enter the Kingdom of God. Everything changed that day two thousand years ago. God poured out His Spirit on those who believed that He had come in the flesh and died for them, had repented, and had been baptized in the name of Jesus Christ for the forgiveness of sin. From that day forward the New Covenant had been established. That is why there is no theology of the thief on the cross- that was before the church age and the outpouring of the Holy Spirit and the establishment of the Kingdom of God on earth. We know nothing of the thief on the cross. We don't know if he was a baptized follower of Jesus Christ and got drunk the night before and stole a donkey. But, we do know that he was under the old covenant. The New Covenant, the Way of God as taught by Jesus, Peter, Philip, and Paul requires belief, repentance, baptism in the name of Jesus, infilling of the Holy Spirit, and to remain in Him.

Since all of the people baptized in the Church in the New Covenant in the book of Acts and in the Epistles were baptized in the name of Jesus, why do most churches baptize in the name of the Father, of the Son, and of the Holy Spirit? Since all people who entered the Church in the Scriptures had to believe, repent, be baptized in the name of Jesus, remain in the Church, and be holy, why do most churches today lower the plan of salvation from Jesus to simple mental assent or attendance?

It is because of false teaching and false doctrine from false teachers, wolves, and false prophets who are unauthorized to teach and teach doctrines of men and traditions of men. This is exactly what Paul was warning the elders of Ephesus about. There has always been a remnant throughout the church age, and there will always be a remnant that bears the truth. Disobedience to the Lord and His Word is what leads to false doctrine.

Once He has revealed to us a truth, we are to be faithful and obedient to Him and His commands.

Who Were Paul and Stephen Willing to Die For?

In Acts 22, the crowd was wanting to kill Paul and rid the earth of him. Who was he willing to die for?

"Then he said: 'The God of our ancestors has chosen you to know His will and to see the Righteous One and to hear words from His mouth. You will be His witness to all people of what you have seen and heard. And now what are you waiting for? Get up, be baptized and wash your sins away, calling on His Name.' "When I returned to Jerusalem and was praying at the temple, I fell into a trance and saw the Lord speaking to me. 'Quick!' He said. 'Leave Jerusalem immediately, because the people here will not accept your testimony about Me.' "'Lord,' I replied, 'these people know that I went from one synagogue to another to imprison and beat those who believe in You. And when the blood of your martyr Stephen was shed, I stood there giving my approval and guarding the clothes of those who were killing him.' (Acts 22:14-19)

Paul describes this persecution and murder perpetrated by false believers upon prophets and even the Messiah in Acts 7:

You stiff-necked people! Your hearts and ears are still uncircumcised. You are just like your ancestors: You always resist the Holy Spirit! Was there ever a prophet your ancestors did not persecute? They even killed those who predicted the coming of the Just One. And now you have betrayed and murdered Him— you who have received the law that was given through angels but have not obeyed it. (Acts 7:51-52)

Paul continues in Acts 22:

"Then the Lord said to me, 'Go; I will send you far away to the Gentiles.'" The crowd listened to Paul until he said this. Then they raised their voices and shouted, **"Rid the earth of him! He's not fit to live!"** (Acts 22:20-22)

Who was Paul and Stephen willing to die for? **Jesus!** Why were they willing to die for Jesus? Because He is God!

There are only four choices we have in understanding who Jesus is:

1. Jesus is God
2. Jesus is Not God
3. Jesus is Another God
4. Jesus is Not Real

We can rule out 'Jesus is Not Real':

Jesus is a historical figure and we have over thirty ancient sources from the time of Jesus from twenty-five different authors who historically confirm that Jesus was real and walked this earth and had a ministry and a following. These authors include Josephus, Tacitus, Pliny the Younger, Suetonius, Philo, and Eusebius.

We can rule out 'Jesus is Not God':

The disciples of Jesus, who were first century monotheistic Jews, worshiped Jesus. A Jew could only worship God, as there was only one God according to the Scriptures.

> *Then she came and **worshiped Him**, saying, "Lord, help me!" (Matthew 15:25)*

> *And as they went to tell His disciples, behold, Jesus met them, saying, "Rejoice!" So they came and held Him by the feet and **worshiped Him**. (Matthew 28:9)*

> *Then the eleven disciples went away into Galilee, to the mountain which Jesus had appointed for them. When they saw Him, **they worshiped Him**; but some doubted. (Matthew 28:16-17)*

Jesus' disciples and apostles called Him God. They all knew there was only one God.

> *Thomas said to Him, **"My Lord and my God!"** Then Jesus told him, "Because you have seen Me, you have believed; blessed are those who have not seen and yet have believed." (John 20:28-29)*

> *For certain individuals whose condemnation was written about long ago have secretly slipped in among you. They are ungodly people, who pervert the grace of our God into a license for immorality and deny **Jesus Christ our only Sovereign and Lord**. Though you already know all this, I want to remind you that **Jesus at one time delivered His people out of Egypt**, but*

> later destroyed those who did not believe. (Jude 4-5)

> Looking for that blessed hope, and the glorious appearing **of our great God and Savior Jesus Christ**; (Titus 2:13)

We Can Rule Out Jesus is Another God:

Although Christianity is monotheistic, believing in only one God, sometimes language slips into bitheism or tritheism, which are both polytheistic. Some people pray to God and then pray to Jesus a different time. We must guard against this, as the God of the Old Testament is clear that He is the only God. As humans, we try to explain this in language sometimes that is confusing to others, using terms such as triune, trinity, persons, persona, manifestation, etc., which can be helpful, but we must understand that there is only one God and there is only one Being, not two or three, and there are not three separate entities that we call God, as that is polytheism. Hear, O Israel, the Lord your God is one.

> Thus says the Lord, the King of Israel and his Redeemer, the Lord of hosts: "I am the first and I am the last; **besides Me there is no god.**" (Isaiah 44:6)

> Fear not, neither be afraid: have not I told you from that time, and have declared it? you are even My witnesses. **Is there a God beside Me? yea, there is no god; I know not any.** (Isaiah 44:8)

*Declare and present your case; let them take counsel together! Who told this long ago? Who declared it of old? Was it not I, the Lord? And **there is no other god besides me**, a righteous God and a Savior; **there is none besides me**. "Turn to me and be saved, all the ends of the earth! For I am God, and there is no other.*** (Isaiah 45:21)

*You are my witnesses," declares the Lord, "and my servant whom I have chosen, that you may know and believe Me and understand that I AM HE. **Before Me no god was formed, nor shall there be any after me.*** (Isaiah 43:10)

*I, I am the Lord, and **besides me there is no savior**.* (Isaiah 43:11)

*To you it was shown, that you might know that **the Lord is God; there is no other besides Him**.* (Deuteronomy 4:35)

*For thus says the Lord, who created the heavens (He is God!), who formed the earth and made it (He established it; He did not create it empty, He formed it to be inhabited!): "**I am the Lord, and there is no other**."* (Isaiah 45:18)

***I am the Lord, and there is no other, besides me there is no God**; I equip you, though you do not know Me,* (Isaiah 45:5)

*Therefore you are great, O Lord God. For there is none like you, and **there is no God besides***

> *you, according to all that we have heard with our ears.* (2 Samuel 7:22)

> *I AM the Lord; that is My Name;* **My glory I give to no other**, *nor my praise to carved idols.* (Isaiah 42:8)

> *See now that **I AM HE; there is no God besides Me**. I bring death and I give life; I wound and I heal, and there is no one who can deliver from My hand.* (Isaiah 45:5)

Jesus is God

The apostles, earliest disciples, and writers of the New Testament believed that Jesus was God in the flesh. This was first century Jewish monotheism. This is the Incarnation. They could only worship God, not another god or a man. They knew God wasn't a compound unity, as is sometimes argued only in the last thirty years, because in Deuteronomy 6:4 God is separating Himself from the pagan gods of the surrounding nations and saying it is only He that is God. The systematic theological Scriptural evidence for Jesus being God, the only true and living God, is overwhelming and easily seen logically. The majority of Biblical scholars today identify Jesus as Yahweh. Why? Because that is what the textual evidence points to. This also explains why the apostles baptized in the Name of Jesus, worshiped Jesus, and were willing to die for Him.

> *And we know that the Son of God has come and has given us understanding, so that we may*

> know Him who is true; and we are in Him who is true, in his Son **Jesus Christ. He is the true God and eternal life**. (1 John 5:20)

> Jesus said to them, "Truly, truly, I say to you, before Abraham was, **I AM**." (John 8:8)

I AM is the name of the God of the Old Testament, and Jesus claims that is who He is and the Pharisees knew He was claiming to be God because they wanted to stone Him for blasphemy for saying that He was God.

> Looking for the blessed hope and glorious appearing of **our great God and Savior Jesus Christ** (Titus 2:13)

Paul understood Jesus to be God and to be the Great God.

> But this I confess unto thee, **that after the Way which they call heresy, so worship I the God of my fathers**, believing all things which are written in the law and in the prophets (Acts 24:14)

As they were charging Paul with worshiping Jesus, he states that He is worshiping the God of their fathers. Even though they are calling it heresy, He is willing to die for worshipping Jesus as God.

> For certain individuals whose condemnation was written about long ago have secretly slipped in among you. They are ungodly people, who pervert the grace of our God into a license for immorality and deny **Jesus Christ our only Sovereign and Lord**. Though you already know

*all this, I want to remind you that **Jesus at one time delivered his people out of Egypt, but later destroyed those who did not believe**.* (Jude 4-5)

Jude writes that Jesus Christ is our only Sovereign and Lord. Jude also states that it was Jesus who delivered the Israelites from Egypt (even though it is Yahweh in the Old Testament) and later destroyed those who did not believe.

God in the New Covenant

  *God the Father

  *Jesus, Son of God, Son of Man

  *Holy Spirit

Isaiah says that Jesus, the Son, is the Everlasting Father.

*For to us a child is born, to us a son is given, and the government will be on his shoulders. And he will be called Wonderful Counselor, Mighty God, **Everlasting Father**, Prince of Peace* (Isaiah 9:6).

Let us examine some of the Scriptural names of God that are also given to Jesus.

Jesus is God: Almighty

God	**Jesus**
Genesis 17:1	Revelation 1:8

Jesus is God: I AM

God	**Jesus**
Exodus 3:14-16	John 8:58

Jesus is God: Horn of Salvation

<u>**God**</u>	<u>**Jesus**</u>
Psalm 18:2	Luke 1:69

Jesus is God: Shepherd

<u>**God**</u>	<u>**Jesus**</u>
Psalm 23:1	John 10:11
Isaiah 40:10-11	Hebrews 13:20
	1 Peter 5:4

Jesus is God: King of Glory

<u>**God**</u>	<u>**Jesus**</u>
Psalm 24:7-10	1 Corinthians 2:8

Jesus is God: Light

God	Jesus
Psalm 27:1	John 1:4-9
Isaiah 60:19	John 8:12
	Revelation 21:23

Jesus is God: Salvation

God	Jesus
Psalm 27:1	Acts 4:10-12
Isaiah 12:2	

Jesus is God: Lord of Lords

God	Jesus
Psalm 136:3	Revelation 19:16

Jesus is God: Holy One

God	Jesus
Isaiah 12:6	Acts 2:27

Jesus is God: Lawgiver

God	**Jesus**
Isaiah 33:22	Hebrews 9:14-17

Jesus is God: Judge

God	**Jesus**
Isaiah 33:22	Micah 5:1
	Acts 10:42

Jesus is God: First and Last

God	**Jesus**
Isaiah 41:4	Revelation 1:8
Isaiah 44:6	Revelation 22:13
Isaiah 48:12	

Jesus is God: Only Savior

God	**Jesus**
Isaiah 43:11	Titus 2:13
Isaiah 45:21	Titus 3:6
Isaiah 60:16	

Jesus is God: Giver of Spiritual Water

God	Jesus
Isaiah 44:3	John 4:10-14
Isaiah 55:1	John 7:38-39

Jesus is God: King of Israel

God	Jesus
Isaiah 44:6	John 1:49
	Revelation 19:16

Jesus is God: Only Creator

God	Jesus
Isaiah 44:24	John 1:3
Isaiah 45:8	Colossians 1:16
Isaiah 48:13	Hebrews 1:10

Jesus is God: Only Just God/Just One

God	Jesus
Isaiah 45:21	Acts 7:52

Jesus is God: Redeemer

God	Jesus
Isaiah 54:5	Galatians 3:13
Isaiah 60:16	Revelation 5:9

If Jesus is the Only True and Living God, how do we reconcile these hard scriptures that seem as though Jesus is a separate entity? How can Jesus be praying to His Father? How can Jesus say His Father is greater than He? Jesus came as fully human and fully God. God, in His humanity, had to eat, drink, walk, suffer, and pray as a human. As God, He still ruled the universe. Both of these attributes, as God and as man, are evident in the Scriptures.

The Dual Nature of Jesus Christ

As a Man, Jesus:	But as God, He:
Was born a baby	Existed from eternity
Luke 2:7	Micah 5:2, John 1:1-2

As a Man, He:	But as God, He:
Grew mentally, physically, spiritually, socially Luke 2:52	Never changes, Hebrews, 13:8

As a Man, He:

Was tempted
by the devil
Luke 4:2

But as God, He:

Cast out devils, Matthew 12:28

As a Man, He:

Hungered
Matthew 4:2

But as God, He:

Was the Bread of Life and
miraculously fed multitudes
John 6:35, Mark 6:38-44, 52

As a Man, He:

Thirsted
John 19:28

But as God, He:

Gave living water
John 4:14

As a Man, He:

Grew weary
John 4:6

But as God, He:

Gave rest Matthew 11:28

As a Man, He:

Slept in a storm
Mark 4:38

But as God, He:

Calmed the storm
Mark 4:39-41

As a Man, He:	**But as God, He:**
Prayed	Answered prayer
Luke 22:41	John 14:14

As a Man, He:	**But as God, He:**
Was scourged and beaten	Healed the sick
John 19:1-3	Matthew 8:16-17
	1 Peter 2:24

As a Man, He:	**But as God, He:**
Died	Raised His own body from the dead
Mark 15:37	John 2:19-21; John 20:9

As a Man, He:	**But as God, He:**
Was a sacrifice for sin	Forgave sin
Hebrews 10:10-12	Mark 2:5-7

As a Man, He:	**But as God, He:**
Did not know all things	Knew all things
Mark 13:32	John 21:17

As a Man, He:	**But as God, He:**
Had no power	Had all power
John 5:30	Matthew 28:18
	Colossians 2:10

As a Man, He:	**But as God, He:**
Was inferior to God	Was equal to God- was God
John 14:28	John 5:18

As a Man, He:	**But as God, He:**
Was a servant	Was King of Kings
Philippians 2:7-8	Revelation 19:16

As we can see with these Scriptures, Jesus is both fully God and fully man. Our creator came in the flesh to suffer and sacrifice for our sins in order to reconcile us to Himself. The Son of Man, Son of God, and Only

Begotten Son are Messianic titles. His Name is Jesus, *I Am Salvation*, and is called Immanuel, *God With Us*, fulfilling the prophecy in Isaiah 7:14.

Salvation and eternal life require belief in Jesus Christ as Lord.

*For God so loved the world, that He gave His only begotten **Son, that whosoever believes in Him** should not perish, but have everlasting life* (John 3:16).

This is the Incarnation, what Christians believe in. God became flesh and dwelt among us, Immanuel (God With Us).

Salvation is found in no one else**, for there **is no other Name** under heaven given to mankind by which we must be **saved (Acts 4:12).

Jesus is the only name we can be saved by.

*He then brought them out and asked, "Sirs, what must I do to be saved?" They replied, **"Believe in the Lord Jesus, and you will be saved**—you and your household." Then they spoke the word of the Lord to him and to all the others in his house. At that hour of the night the jailer took them and washed their wounds; then **immediately he and all his household were baptized*** (Acts 16:30-33).

Only belief in Jesus leads to salvation. Belief in God doesn't, unless you believe Jesus is God. Belief in another God doesn't. Only belief in Jesus and that He is

God leads to salvation. Note that the jailer and all his household were **baptized immediately**, as was everyone else in the Book of Acts. There was no waiting for a baptismal day or a baptism picnic or until the weather was better. Believers were baptized in water immediately.

If you declare with your mouth, "Jesus is Lord," and believe in your heart that God raised him from the dead, you will be saved. For it is with your heart that you believe and are justified, and it is with your mouth that you profess your faith and are saved (Romans 10:9-10)

Declaration of Jesus is Lord is required for salvation. Paul wrote this to the believers in Rome that were already baptized (Romans 6) and filled with the Holy Spirit (Romans 8). This belief and confession were the two bases of the Roman believers fully obeying Jesus and being baptized and filled with His Spirit.

*Whoever **believes in the Son** has eternal life; whoever does not obey the Son shall not see life, but the wrath of God remains on him* (John 3:36).

One must believe in Jesus to be saved and one who does not obey Jesus shall not see eternal life.

*But as many as received **Him**, to them gave He power to become the children of God, even to them that believe on **His Name**: Which were born, not of blood, nor of the will of the flesh, nor of the will of man, but of God* (John 1:12-13).

John says that belief in the Name of Jesus is required to become the children of God. This is the Name of God. This is HaShem, the Name.

No one who denies the Son has the Father; whoever acknowledges the Son has the Father also (1 John 2:23).

John doubles down and says that if you deny the Son you do not have the Father and if you acknowledge the Son you have the Father. Belief in Jesus is what is needed to have salvation and reconciliation with God.

Jesus is God

There are numerous examples of Jesus fulfilling what YAHWEH describes as Himself in the Old Testament. Let us just examine a few in the following pages.

Jesus is God: Provider

God	**Jesus**
Yahweh-jireh	Provider
	Hebrews 10:10-12

Yahweh describes Himself as the God Who Provides in the Hebrew Scriptures, where Jesus is described as the Provider in Hebrews 10. Jesus provides the sacrifice for our sins, making us holy, fulfilling the Lord's promise to Abraham that 'God will provide Himself a lamb for sacrifice.'

Jesus is God: Healer

God	Jesus
Yahweh-rapha	Healer James 5:14-15

In the Hebrew Scriptures, Yahweh describes Himself as the God Who Heals. James describes Jesus as the One Who Heals when he says:

Is there anyone among you sick? Let them call the elders of the church to pray over them and anoint them with oil in the Name of the Lord. And the prayer offered in faith will make the sick person well; the Lord will raise them up." (James 5:14-15)

Jesus is God: Victory

God	Jesus
Yahweh-nissi	Victory
(Banner, Victory)	1 Corinthians 15:57

Yahweh is our victory in the Old Testament, but Paul says that Jesus gives us our victory when he writes to the Corinthians.

Jesus is God: Sanctifier

God	Jesus
Yahweh-mkaddesh	Sanctifier
Sanctifier	Ephesians 5:26

The Hebrew scriptures identify Yahweh as the sanctifier, but Paul identifies Jesus as the sanctifier when he writes to the Ephesians:

Husbands, love your wives, just as Christ loved the church and gave Himself up for her to make her holy, cleansing her by the washing with water through the Word, and to present her to Himself as a radiant church, without stain or wrinkle or any other blemish, but holy and blameless. (Ephesians 5:25-26)

Jesus is God: Peace

God	**Jesus**
Yahweh-shalom	Peace
Peace	John 14:27

Yahweh identifies Himself as the God of Peace, but Jesus identifies Himself with peace in the book of John:

Peace I leave with you, My peace I give you. (John 14:27)

Jesus is God: Lord of Hosts

God	**Jesus**
Yahweh-Sabaoth	Lord of Hosts
Lord of Hosts	

Thus says the LORD, the King and Redeemer of Israel, the LORD of hosts: 'I am the first and I am the last; besides me there is no god' (Isaiah 44:6).

These shall make war with the Lamb, and the Lamb shall overcome them: for he is Lord of lords, and King of kings: and they that are with him are called, and chosen, and faithful (Revelation 17:14).

Jesus is God: Most High

God	**Jesus**
Yahweh-elon	Most High
Most High	Luke 1:32, Luke 1:76
	Luke 1:78

Jesus is God: Shepherd

God	**Jesus**
Yahweh-raah	Shepherd
Shepherd	John 10:11

Whereas Yahweh says that He is the Shepherd, Jesus identifies Himself as the Good Shepherd.

I am the good shepherd. The good shepherd lays down his life for the sheep (John 10:11).

Jesus is God: Maker

God	Jesus
Yahweh-hoseenu	Maker
Maker	John 1:3

John 1:3 is a foundational verse in Christianity, stating that "All things were made through Him, and without Him was not any thing made that was made," referring to Jesus Christ (the Word or Logos), establishing His divine role as the agent of all creation, with no exception. This verse, following John 1:1-2 which identifies the Word with God, highlights Jesus's pre-existence and essential involvement in bringing everything into existence, emphasizing His uniqueness and power over the cosmos.

Jesus is God: Righteousness

God	Jesus
Yahweh-tsidkenu	Righteousness
Righteousness	1 Corinthians 1:30

*It is because of him that you are **in Christ Jesus**, who has become for us wisdom from God—that is, **our righteousness**, holiness and redemption* (1 Corinthians 1:30).

1 Corinthians 1:30 says that believers are in Christ Jesus because of God, and Christ has become their divine provision for wisdom, righteousness, holiness, and

redemption, meaning He gives them right standing with God, purity, and freedom from sin. It's a core verse explaining how Christ fulfills all spiritual needs for believers, becoming their source of truth, justification, sanctification, and deliverance.

The key meanings in 1 Corinthians 1:30:

1. "In Christ Jesus": Believers are united with Him, deriving their identity and life from Him, and this union occurs at baptism, according to Scripture. "In Christ" means baptized into Him.
2. Wisdom from God: Christ is God's perfect revelation and guidance, the ultimate source of true understanding.
3. Righteousness: Christ makes believers right with God, giving them a righteous status they couldn't earn.
4. Holiness (Sanctification): He sets believers apart, making them pure and holy.
5. Redemption: He frees them from the bondage and penalty of sin.

Jesus is God: Ever Present One

God	**Jesus**
Yahweh-shammah	Ever Present One
Present	Matthew 28:20

*And teaching them to obey everything I have commanded you. And **surely I am with you always**, to the very end of the age* (Matthew 28:20).

Jesus has promised to be with us always, to be ever present with us. How does He do this? He gives us His Holy Spirit!

The Jews did not understand how God could come in flesh. They did not understand Jesus on one occasion when He told them He was the Father (John 8:19-27). However, on many other occasions they did understand His claim to be God. Once when Jesus healed a man on the Sabbath and credited the work to His Father, the Jews sought to kill Him- not only because He had broken the Sabbath but because He said God was His Father, making Himself equal with God.

From the Scriptures, We Know:

>**God is Spirit**
>
>**There is but One God**
>
>**Jesus is God**
>
>**Jesus is Man**

Since we know the Scriptures, let us examine those that demonstrate that God and Jesus are One.

We Know:

God is Coming	**Jesus is Coming**
Zechariah 14:4,5	1 Thessalonians 3:11-13
1 Thessalonians 4:13-18	Matthew 25:31-46
Revelation 19:11,16	Titus 2:11-13
Psalm 50:1-6	

Jesus is God: Judge

God	**Jesus**
Isaiah 33:22	Micah 5:1
	Acts 10:42

Stephen and Paul died because they believed Jesus WAS God. They did not get martyred because they thought He was another God. Plenty of pagan Greeks and romans believed in many gods but were not stoned or beheaded or crucified because of it. We must teach the world and Christians that Jesus is the only Name that can save them.

I told you that you would die in your sins; if you do not believe that I AM HE, you will indeed die in your sins (John 8:24).

Jesus plainly says that if one does not believe that He is God, they will indeed die in their sins.

Jesus is God

As a Man, Jesus:	But as God, He:
Jesus wept.	Wipes away our tears.
John 11:35	Revelation 21:4
Luke 19:41	
Hebrews 5:7-9	

Who in the days of His flesh*, when He had offered up prayers and supplications with **strong crying and tears*** (Hebrews 5:7).

Jesus was God in the flesh. He came as God With Us, Emmanuel. This is the Incarnation, God in the flesh. As a man, He cried, just as we do. Notice that He cried in prayer.

He will wipe away every tear *from their eyes, and death shall be no more, neither shall there be mourning, nor crying, nor pain anymore, for the former things have passed away* (Revelation 21:4).

Jesus, as God, will wipe away every tear. In the days of His flesh, He cried. As God, He wipes away our tears.

Come on, Saints! God wants you to seek His Face! Paul said he only wants to know Him! Seek the Living God while you still can!

Who is God?

God is a Spirit

The Scriptures reveal that God is a Spirit in John 4:23-24; Acts 7:48-49; Acts 17:24-28; Psalm 139:7-12; 1 Kings 8:27; and Jeremiah 23:23-24.

There is But One God

From Scripture we can see that **there is but One God** according to Deuteronomy 6:4-9; Mark 12:28-32; Malachi 2:10; Isaiah 44:6-8; Isaiah 45:2-6; Isaiah 45:21-23; Isaiah 46:8-9; 1 Corinthians 8:4-6; Ephesians 4:5-6; 1 Timothy 2:5; James 2:19; and Revelation 4:2-3.

Jesus is God

That **Jesus is God** is a foundational principle of classical Christianity and Biblical Christianity based on the Scriptures. We can see that Jesus is God according to Isaiah 7:14; Isaiah 9:6; Micah 5:2; John 1:1; John 1:14; John 1:10; John 8:24; John 8:58-59; John 14:6-11; 2 Corinthians 5:19; 1 Timothy 3:16.

Jesus is Man

We also see in the Scriptures that Jesus is man according to Isaiah 7:14; Isaiah 90:6; Luke 1:31; Luke 2:6-7; Acts 17:31; Galatians 4:4; Philippians 2:7-8; 1 Timothy 2:5; Hebrews 4:15; Hebrews 7:24-25.

That Jesus is God is a basic foundational principle of monotheistic Christianity and aligns with First Century Jewish monotheism and First Century Church as revealed in the New Testament.

One Creator

We know that there is only one God and the Scriptures reveal **God the Creator** and **Jesus the Creator**. **God as Creator is revealed** in Genesis 1:1; Genesis 2:7; Job 33:4; Psalm 33:6; Psalm 104:30; Isaiah 40:28; Isaiah 44:24; Isaiah 45:11-18; and Malachi 2:10. **Jesus is revealed as the Creator** in John 1:10; 1 Corinthians 8:6; Ephesians 3:9; Colossians 1:12-17; Hebrews 1:8-12; Revelation 4:8-11; Revelation 10:6; Revelation 14:6-7; Revelation 21:5-7; and Revelation 22:3.

One Savior

We know that there is only one God and the Scriptures reveal **God as the Redeemer and Savior and Jesus as the Redeemer and Savior**. **God as Savior is revealed** in Psalm 78:34,35; Isaiah 47:4; Isaiah 44:6; Isaiah 43:3-11; Isaiah 45:21, Isaiah 49:26; Psalm 106:21; and Luke 1:46-47. **Jesus is revealed as the Redeemer and Savior** in 1 John 4:14; 1 Peter 2:21-24; Acts 20:28; Galatians 3:13; Luke 24:21-29; Luke 2:10-11; John 4:40-42; Philippians 3:20; 1 Timothy 1:1-3; 1 Timothy 4:10; Titus 1:1-4; Titus 2:10-13; 1 Peter 1:10, 11; and Jude 25.

One Shepherd

We know that there is only one God and the Scriptures reveal **God the Shepherd and Jesus the Shepherd**. **God as Shepherd** is revealed in Psalm 23; Isaiah 40:10, 11; and Psalm 100. **Jesus is revealed as the Shepherd** in John 10:8-12; 1 Peter 2:21-25; Hebrews 13:20; and 1 Peter 5:4.

One King

We know that there is only one God and the Scriptures reveal **God the King and Jesus the King. God is revealed as King** in Psalm 24; Psalm 44:4; Psalm 74:12; Isaiah 43:10-15; Isaiah 44:6-8; Jeremiah 10:10; and Zechariah 14:9. **Jesus is revealed as the King** in Matthew 2:1-6; Luke 19:32-38; Luke 23:3; John 18:37; John 19-21; 1 Timothy 6:13-16; Revelation 15:1-4; and Revelation 19:11-16.

One I AM

We know that there is only one God and the Scriptures reveal **God as I AM and Jesus as I AM. God is revealed as I AM** in Exodus 3:13, 14; Isaiah 43:10-11; and Isaiah 43:25. **Jesus is revealed as I AM** in John 18:5-8; Revelation 1:17-18; and John 8:24-28.

One First and Last

We know that there is only one God and the Scriptures reveal **God as First and Last and Jesus as First and Last. God is revealed as First and Last** in Isaiah 41:4; Isaiah 43:10-11; and Isaiah 44:6, 8. **Jesus is revealed as First and Last** in Revelation 1:17 and Revelation 22:13.

One Rock

We know that there is only one God and the Scriptures reveal **God as the Rock and Jesus as the Rock. God is revealed as the Rock** in Deuteronomy 32:1-4; 2 Samuel 22:1-3; 2 Samuel 22:32; Psalm 18:2; Psalm 31:3; Psalm 78:34-35; Psalm 89:26; and Isaiah 17:10-11. **Jesus is revealed as the Rock** in Matthew 16:17-19; Isaiah

28:16; Acts 4:11-12; 1 Corinthians 10:4; Numbers 20:1-11; Ephesians 2:20-22; and 1 Peter 2:6-8.

One is Coming

We know that there is only one God and the Scriptures reveal **God is Coming and Jesus is Coming. God is revealed as Coming** in Zechariah 14:4,5; 1 Thessalonians 4:13-18; Revelation 19:11, 16; and Psalm 50:1-6. **Jesus is revealed as Coming** in 1 Thessalonians 3:11-13; Matthew 25:31-46; and Titus 2:11-13.

Based on the above Scriptural analysis there is only One God, and He came in the flesh and revealed Himself as God with Us, I AM Salvation, and walked with us as the only image of God we can see and was fully God and fully man.

† The Revelation of Jesus Christ

The Book of Revelation is the Revelation of Jesus Christ. This book reveals who Jesus Christ is and what He is doing. The following is a list of Jesus Christ as revealed to us in the Book of The Revelation of Jesus Christ.

Faithful Witness (1:5)

First Born of the dead (1:5)

King of Kings (1:5)

Alpha and Omega (1:8, 11; 21:6; 22:13)

Beginning and End (1:8; 21:6; 22:13)

One Which Is, Was, Is To Come (1:8; 4:8)

The Almighty (1:8; 4:8)

Son of Man (1:13)

First and Last (1:17; 22:13)

He that Lives, was Dead, is Alive for Evermore (1:18)

Possessor of Seven Spirits (3:1; 5:6)

One on the Throne (4:2)

God (4:8; 21:7)

Creator (4:11)

Lion of Tribe of Judah (5:5)

Root of David (5:5; 22:16)

Lamb (5:6)

Redeemer (5:9)

Faithful (19:11)

True (19:11)

The Word of God (19:13)

King of Kings (19:16)

Lord of Lords (19:16)

Offspring of David (22:16)

Bright and Morning Star (22:16)

Each of these titles and roles is a beautiful revelation of Jesus. Together, they present a portrait of One who came in flesh, died, and rose again but also One who is the everlasting Lord God Almighty.

No longer will there be any curse. The throne of God and of the Lamb will be in the city, and His servants will serve Him. They will see His face, and His Name will be on their foreheads. (Revelation 22:3-4)

The last chapter of Revelation **describes God and the Lamb in the singular** (Revelation 22:3-4) and **identifies the Lord God of the holy prophets as Jesus** (Revelation 22:6,16) These references tell us that Jesus is the God of eternity and that He will appear with His glorified human body (the Lamb) throughout eternity.

The angel said to me, "These words are trustworthy and true. **The Lord, the God who inspires the prophets, sent**

His angel *to show His servants the things that must soon take place."* (Revelation 22:6).

I, Jesus, have sent my angel *to give you this testimony for the churches. I am the Root and the Offspring of David, and the bright Morning Star.* (Revelation 22:16)

These two verses show that **Jesus is the God who inspires the prophets and sent His angel** to tell His servants of the things that must soon take place.

Bright and Morning Star (22:16)

God's glory will be the light for the New Jerusalem as it shines through the glorified body of Jesus (Revelation 21:23.

*They called to the mountains and the rocks, "Fall on us and hide us from the face of Him who sits on the throne and from the wrath of the Lamb? For the great day of **His** wrath has come, and who can withstand it?"* (Revelation 6:16,17).

The earliest manuscripts and all translations for 1800 years utilized the singular 'His' in Revelation 6:17, implying that the Lamb is the One who sits on the throne. Later manuscripts and translations changed 'His' to 'theirs', attempting to imply a duality or plurality of gods.

These closing chapters of the book of Revelation describes how God will reveal (unveil) Himself in all His glory to everyone forever. They tell us that Jesus is the everlasting God and that Jesus will reveal Himself as

God throughout eternity. Therefore, the book is indeed the revelation of Jesus Christ.

Jesus and His Followers Do Claim that He is God:

I AM

God said to Moses, "**I AM that I AM**." And He said, "You must say this to the Israelites, '**I AM** has sent me to you." (Exodus 3:14)

Jesus said to them, "I tell you the solemn truth, before Abraham came into existence, **I AM**!" (John 8:58)

Jesus' name literally means I AM SALVATION.

The Lord Will Provide (Jireh)

And Abraham called the name of that place "The Lord provides." It is said to this day, "In the mountain of the Lord provision will be made." (Genesis 22:14) (God will provide Himself a lamb for sacrifice)

On the next day John saw Jesus coming toward him and said, "Look, the Lamb of God Who takes away the sin of the world!" (John 1:29)

The Name

"For from the east to the west **My Name** will be great among the nations. Incense and pure offerings will be offered in **My Name** everywhere, for **My Name** will be great among the nations." says the Lord who rules over all. (Malachi 1:11)

Therefore go and make disciples of all nations, baptizing them in **The Name** of the Father and the Son and the Holy Spirit, teaching them to obey everything I have commanded you. And remember, I AM with you always, to the end of the age. (Matthew 28:19-20)

Therefore God exalted Him to the highest place and gave Him the Name that is above all names, that at the **Name of Jesus** every knee should bow, in heaven and on earth and under the earth, and every tongue acknowledge that Jesus Christ is Lord, to the glory of God the Father. (Philippians 2:9-11)

The Lord is My Shepherd

The Lord is my shepherd, I shall not want. (Psalm 23:1)

I am the Good Shepherd. The Good Shepherd lays down His life for the sheep. (John 10:11)

The Alpha and Omega

God as Yahweh calls himself the beginning and the end in Isaiah.

Who acts and carries out decrees? Who summons the successive generations from the beginning? I, the Lord, am present at the very beginning, and at the very end- I am the one. (Isaiah 41:4)

Jesus is identified as the First and the Last in the book of Revelation.

I am the Alpha and the Omega, says the Lord God- the one who is, and who was, and who is still to come- the All-Powerful! (Revelation 1:8)

He also said to me, "It is done! I am the Alpha and the Omega, the beginning and the end. To the one who is thirsty I will give water free of charge from the spring of the water of life." (Revelation 21:6)

I am the Alpha and the Omega, the first and the last, the beginning and the end! (Revelation 22:13)

Father

Yet, Lord, you are our Father. We are the clay, and You are our Potter; we are all the product of Your labor. (Isaiah 64:8)

For you did not receive the spirit of slavery leading again to fear, but you received the Spirit of adoption, by whom we cry, "Abba, Father." (Romans 8:15)

For unto us a child is born, unto us a Son is given; and the government shall be upon His shoulder, and His name shall be called Wonderful Counselor, Mighty God, Everlasting Father, Prince of Peace. (Isaiah 9:6)

Rock

*As for **the Rock**, His work is perfect, for all His ways are just. **He is a reliable God** who is never unjust, He is fair and upright. (Deuteronomy 32:4)*

*He only is **my Rock and my salvation**, my stronghold; I shall not be shaken. On God my salvation and my glory rest; the **rock of my strength**, my refuge is in God. (Psalm 62:6-7)*

*Are you not **from everlasting, O Lord, my God, my Holy One**? We will not die. You, O Lord, have appointed* them to judge; and **You, O Rock**, have established them to correct. (Habakkuk 1:12)

*And all drank from the same spiritual drink. For they were all drinking from the spiritual Rock that followed them, and **the Rock was Christ**.* (1 Corinthians 10:4)

Jesus is Identified as God

*I and the Father are **one**.* (John 10:10)

*You must have the same attitude that **Christ Jesus** had. **Though He was God**, He did not think of equality with God as something to cling to.*

***In Him dwells the fullness of the Godhead bodily**, and in Christ you have been brought to fullness. He is the head over every power and authority.* (Colossians 2:9-10)

*We are not stoning you for any good work, they replied, but for blasphemy, because **you, a mere man, claim to be God**.* (John 10:33)

*In the beginning was the Word, and the Word was with God, and **the Word was God…And the Word became flesh and dwelt among us**, and we have seen His glory, glory as of the only Son from the Father, full of grace and truth.* (John 1:1,14)

*The people said, "You aren't even fifty years old. How can you say you have seen Abraham?" Jesus answered, "I tell you the truth, before Abraham was even born, **I AM!**"* (John 8:57-58)

This made the Jews ask, "Will He kill Himself? Is that why He says, 'Where I go, you cannot come'? But He continued, "You are from below; I am from above. You are from this world; I am not of this world. I told you that you would die in your sins; **if you do not believe that I AM HE***, you will indeed die in your sins."* (John 8:22-24)

I am not referring to all of you; I know those I have chosen. But this is to fulfill this passage of Scripture: 'He who shared my bread has turned against me.' "I am tell you now before it happens, so that when it does happen you will believe that **I AM WHO I AM**.*"* (John 13:18-19)

Thus says the Lord, the King of Israel and his Redeemer, the Lord of Hosts: "I am the first and I am the last; besides me there is no god." (Isaiah 44:6)

And to the angel of the church in Smyrna write: 'The words of **the First and Last, who died and came to life**.*'* (Revelation 2:8)

When I saw Him, I fell at His feet as though dead. But He laid His right hand on me, saying, "Fear not, **I am the First and the Last, and the living one. I died, and behold I am alive forevermore***, and I have keys of death and Hades."* (Revelation 1:17-18)

Only God Can Be Worshipped

After Jesus was born in Bethlehem in Judea, during the time of King Herod, Magi from the east came to Jerusalem and asked, "Where is the One who has been born King of the Jews? We saw His star when it rose have come **to worship Him**.*"* (Matthew 2:1-2)

So the women hurried away from the tomb, afraid yet filled with joy, and ran to tell His disciples. Suddenly Jesus met them. "Greetings," He said. They came to Him, clasped His feet and **worshiped Him**. (Matthew 28:8-9)

Then the eleven disciples went to Galilee, to the mountain where Jesus had told them to go. When they saw him, **they worshiped Him**; *but some doubted.* (Matthew 28:16-17)

Jesus is Prayed to, Revealing that He is God

And as they were stoning Stephen, he called out, "Lord Jesus, receive my spirit." And falling to his knees he cried out with a loud voice, "Lord, do not hold this sin against them." (Acts 7:59-60)

Then He said to Thomas, "Put your finger here; see my hands. Reach out your hand and put it into my side. Stop doubting and believe." Thomas said to Him, **"My Lord and my God."** (John 20:27-28)

Simeon Peter, a servant and apostle of Jesus Christ, to those who have obtained a faith of equal standing with ours by the righteousness of **our God and Savior Jesus Christ**. (2 Peter 1:1)

You are My witnesses, says the Lord, and my servant whom I have chosen, that you may know and believe Me, and understand **that I am He. Before Me there was no God formed, nor shall there be after Me**. *I, even I, am the Lord, and* **besides Me there is no savior**. *I have declared and saved, I have proclaimed, and there was no foreign god among you, therefore you are My* *witnesses, says the Lord, that I AM God*. (Isaiah 43:10-12)

That Jesus is God is a fundamental and sound doctrine of Christianity. The Lord, Peter, John, and Paul teach us that this understanding is a core concept of salvation and being reconciled to God. There is no other path to eternity and entering the Kingdom of God. This is so important that Paul doubles down on it in Acts 20:

Keep watch over yourselves and all the flock *of which the Holy Spirit has made you overseers. Be shepherds of the* **church of God, which He bought with His own blood**. (Acts 20:28)

Jesus shed His blood for us, and Paul says that God bought His church with His own blood. Jesus is God, and this understanding and confession is necessary for salvation.

Dear friends, do not believe every spirit, but test the spirits to see whether they are from God, because many false prophets have gone out into the world. This is how you can recognize the Spirit of God: **Every spirit that acknowledges that Jesus Christ has come in the flesh is from God**, *but every spirit that does not acknowledge Jesus is not from God. This is the spirit of the antichrist, which you have heard is coming and even now is already in the world* (1 John 4:1-3).

This verse says that every spirit that acknowledges **that I AM SALVATION The ANOINTED ONE** has come in the flesh is from God and those that do not are the spirit of antichrist, which is anything that is against Christ, including the knowledge of His deity.

*Until I come, **devote yourself to the public reading of Scripture, to preaching and to doctrine**. Do not neglect your gift, which was given you through prophecy when the body of elders laid their hands on you. Be diligent in these matters; give yourself wholly to them, so that everyone may see your progress. **Watch your life and doctrine closely. Persevere in them, because if you do, you will save both yourself and your hearers**.* (1 Timothy 4:13-16)

Devote yourself to doctrine, sound doctrine, not what is sold as doctrine. Be diligent and give yourself wholly to sound doctrine, so that everyone may see your progress. Watch your life and doctrine closely and persevere in them so that you will save yourself and your hearers. Sound doctrine leads to salvation.

God is Light

*This is the message we have heard from Him and announce to you, that **God is Light**, and in Him there is no darkness at all.* (1 John 1:5)

Jesus is Light

*Again **Jesus** spoke to them, saying, "**I AM the light of the world**. Whoever follows me will not walk in darkness, but will have the light of life.* (John 8:12)

We are Light

You are the light of the world. *A town built on a hill cannot be hidden. Neither do people light a lamp and put it under a bowl. Instead they put it on its stand, and it gives light to everyone in the house. In the same way,* ***let your light shine*** *before others, that they may see your good deeds and glorify your Father in heaven.* (Matthew 5:14-16)

Jesus is light, but because He now dwells in believers, He has made us light, and we are to put on the Armor of Light, which is Christ Jesus.

The Omniscient God

In Job chapter 38, the Lord shows up and speaks to Job and his friends:

1 Then the Lord spoke to Job out of the storm. He said:

The Lord finally answers Job, after His long silence. Job could not respond to Elihu, since he knew Elihu's charges were false, yet Elihu claimed to be speaking for God. Job would have to leave the answer with God.

2 Who is this that obscures my plans with words without knowledge?

God is rebuking Elihu and Job. The latter has not been speaking, but Elihu has been mouthing 'words without knowledge' for the equivalent of six chapters and 165 verses. Who is this that questions my wisdom and authority with such ignorant words? Why do you talk so much when you know so little?

Paul levels the same charge to Timothy against many false teachers who have already come into Ephesus shortly after Paul left:

They want to be teachers of the law, but they do not know what they are talking about or what they so confidently affirm (1 Timothy 1:7).

Just like in the days of Job and in the days of Paul, there are many teachers who do not know nor teach sound doctrine as defined by Jesus, Peter, John, and Paul in the Scriptures. If Peter or Paul showed up at your church today and asked if you were baptized and you said 'no,' they would immediately take you to be baptized. If Paul or Peter or John showed up at your church today and asked if you had received the Holy Spirit and you hadn't or didn't know, they would baptize you and lay hands on you to receive the Holy Spirit. Paul tells Timothy that these teachers do not know what they are talking about, even though they feel confident about what they are teaching is correct. Many people are teaching doctrine that they believe is correct, but it is not sound doctrine that heals, saves, and makes you whole. One may deeply dig into the Bible and preach fervently, like Apollos was, but still not be teaching sound doctrine as taught by Jesus, Peter, John, and Paul as is revealed in the Scriptures.

God and His Identification

Great are the works of the Lord, studied by all who delight in them. (Psalm 111:2)

Theology is the study of God. Without faith it is impossible to please God, because you must first believe that He exists, and is a rewarder of those who seek Him diligently. Our goal should be to seek Him, study Him, and reflect upon Him and His Word.

Paul said that His desire was to know Him:

All I want is to know Christ *and to experience the power of his resurrection, to share in His sufferings and become like Him in his death* (Philippians 3:10).

*Beloved, now **we are children of God**, and what we will be has not yet been made known. But we know that **when Christ appears, we shall be like Him, for we shall see Him as He is*** (1 John 3:2).

This is our future transformation. This verse promises that believers will experience a complete transformation, becoming like Christ in a glorified state when He returns.

We will be seeing Him as He is. The reason for this transformation is the direct vision of God; we can't see Him in our current state but will have glorified bodies to behold His full glory.

We are to live holy lives in hope and purity. The hope of this future likeness motivates believers to live pure and holy lives now, purifying themselves as He is pure.

As for me, I will behold Your face in righteousness; I shall be satisfied, when I awake, with seeing Your likeness (Psalm 17:15).

† Fulfillment

The Greek word ***tetelestai*** was used by Jesus on the cross, signifying completion, finished, and ultimate fulfillment. Jesus' cry on the cross signifies complete accomplishment and fulfillment of God's plan, a profound conclusion. What was completed? The completion of God's purpose and promises, leading to ultimate hope and restoration to God.

Let us hear the conclusion of the whole matter: fear God, and keep His commandments: for this is the whole duty of mankind (Ecclesiastes 12:13).

Jesus had both divine self-consciousness and human self-consciousness but not two centers of consciousness. Jesus did not have two spirits, but deity and humanity were joined in His Spirit.

Jesus is the Holy One of Israel in the Midst of Isaiah 12

*In that day you will say: "I will praise you, LORD. Although You were angry with me, Your anger has turned away and You have comforted me. Surely **God is my salvation**; I will trust and not be afraid. The LORD, the LORD Himself, is my strength and my defense**; He has become my salvation**." With joy you will draw water from the wells of salvation. In that day you will say: "Give praise to the LORD, proclaim **His Name**; make known among the nations what He has done, and proclaim that **His Name is exalted**. Sing to the LORD, for He has done glorious things; let this be known to all the world. Shout aloud and sing for joy, people of Zion,* *for great is **the Holy One** of Israel among you."* (Isaiah 12:1-6)

The verse, 'God is my salvation,' is actually the name of Jesus. His Name is God is My Salvation. His Name, Jesus, is the Name that we proclaim and the Name that we exalt. He is the Holy One of Israel.

God was in Christ, Reconciling the World to Himself

*Now the **One who has fashioned us for this very purpose is God**, who has given us the **Spirit** as a deposit, guaranteeing what is to come* (2 Corinthians 5:5).

Paul tells the Corinthians that God has designed us for a heavenly body and home and our spirit groans for this life.

*Since, then, we know what it is to **fear the Lord**, we try to persuade others. What we are is plain to God, and I hope it is also plain to your conscience* (2 Corinthians 5:11).

Paul then explains to the Corinthian Church what it means to fear the Lord, and that we are to persuade others.

*Therefore, if anyone is **in Christ, the new creation has come**: The old has gone, the new is here* (2 Corinthians 5:17)!

Paul has in multiple passages shown us that to be IN CHRIST is to be baptized IN CHRIST. Our old man is washed away and the new creation is here.

All this is from God, who reconciled us to Himself through Christ and gave us the ministry of reconciliation: **that God was in Christ reconciling the world to Himself**, *not counting people's sins against them. And He has committed to us the message of reconciliation* (2 Corinthians 5:18-19).

Paul tells the repentant, baptized, and Holy Spirit-filled Corinthian church that God was in Christ, reconciling the world to Himself. This is the Incarnation: God in the flesh! He is Emmanuel, God with us! In Him dwelt the fullness of the Godhead in the flesh! He is the express image of God, the only way we could see God in the flesh. Paul then reminds us that we have been commissioned to spread the message of reconciliation to God.

We are therefore Christ's ambassadors, as though God were making his appeal through us. We implore you on Christ's behalf: Be reconciled to God. God made him who had no sin to be sin for us, so that in him we might become the righteousness of God (2 Corinthians 5:20-21).

Unlike us, Jesus had no sin, for He came in human identity as God in the flesh, not fallen humanity.

But you know that **He was manifested** *to take away our sins. And in Him is no sin* (1 John 3:5).

Jesus is God manifested in the flesh, sinless, and shed His (God's) blood for us according to Paul and Luke, as Paul bid farewell and prayed for the Ephesian elders as he gave them the sound doctrine charge.

*Keep watch over yourselves and all the flock of which the Holy Spirit has made you overseers. Be shepherds of the church of **God, which He bought with His own blood*** (Acts 20:28).

To redeem fallen humanity, God came in human identity as Jesus Christ, the Son of God. Jesus is one personal being, who is both God and human at the same time. Deity and humanity are united in Him. God was manifested in the flesh as Jesus (1 Timothy 3:16). The Word (the self-revealing God) was made flesh (John 1:14). In these verses, flesh doesn't mean merely a body, but full humanity. Jesus was fully human, with everything that makes us human, including body, soul, spirit, mind, and will, with one integrated personality that united deity and humanity, as can be seen in the following three verses (Bernard, 2025).

*Then he said to them, "My **soul** is overwhelmed with **sorrow** to the point of death. Stay here and keep watch with me." Going a little farther, he fell with his face to the ground and prayed, "My Father, if it is possible, may this cup be taken from me. Yet not as I **will**, but as you will."* (Matthew 26:38-39).

*Jesus called out with a loud **voice**, "Father, into your hands I commit my **spirit**."[a] When he had said this, he **breathed** his last.* (Luke 23:46).

*Since the children have **flesh and blood, He too shared in their humanity** so that by His death He might break the power of him who holds the power of death—that is, the devil— and free those who all their lives were held in slavery by their fear of death. For surely it is not* *angels He helps, but Abraham's descendants. For this reason **He had to be made like them, fully human in every way**, in order that He might become a merciful and faithful high priest in service to God, and that He might make atonement for the sins of the people. Because He Himself **suffered** when He was **tempted**, He is able to help those who are being tempted.* (Hebrews 2:14-18)

True scriptural understanding of who Jesus is and the Way of God to enter into His Kingdom is precisely what Jesus and the apostles wrote, not what councils and creeds and denominations and later history have decided. This theology of who Jesus is and what is the route of salvation are consistent with basic Christianity. God became flesh and dwelt among us, and poured out His Spirit upon us.

† Conclusion of the Whole Matter

Let us hear the conclusion of the whole matter: Fear God, and keep His commandments (Ecclesiastes 12:13).

In Ecclesiastes we see life's purpose as fearing God and keeping His commands, highlighting the final result of wisdom.

After Paul had seen the vision, we got ready at once to leave for Macedonia, concluding that God had called us to preach the Gospel to them (Acts 16:9-10).

Paul and his companions (Luke, Silas, Timothy) decide to go to Macedonia after Paul sees a vision of a man pleading, 'Come over into Macedonia, and help us,' concluding God called them to preach the Gospel there, marking a shift in their missionary journey from Asia to Europe, as they were previously prevented from going to Asia by the Holy Spirit. Immediately after Paul had the vision in Troas of a man from Macedonia begging him to come and bring the Gospel to them, he and his entourage set out for Macedonia, understanding this as a divine call to evangelize the Europeans. God uses His Spirit to direct us in our ministry work, even when our own plans are thwarted.

The Greek word for 'concluding' in Acts 16:10 is *sumbibazo*, meaning 'to bring together', 'concluding', or 'assuredly gathering.' Let us bring together and conclude what the sound doctrine that Paul was teaching.

*Join with others in following my example, brothers and sisters. Pay close attention to those who live in **keeping with the pattern we gave you*** (Philippians 3:17).

There is a pattern that Paul was teaching, and it was the Way that Jesus and the other apostles were teaching. This is the sound doctrine that we can trace that Paul was teaching.

***Finally**, brothers and sisters, whatever is true, whatever is noble, whatever is right, whatever is pure, whatever is lovely, whatever is admirable- if anything is excellent or praiseworthy- think about such things. **Whatever you have learned or received or heart from me, or seen in me- PUT IT INTO PRACTICE**. And the God of peace will be with you* (Philippians 4:8-9).

Paul was teaching and charging the elders at Ephesus and Timothy and Titus to **teach sound doctrine**. This sound doctrine is teaching that heals or makes you whole and gives us salvation. The word translated as salvation also means to heal or make whole, like a healing salve that we apply to a wound or lesion. The words 'salvation' and 'salve' come from the same root 'to heal or make whole.'

It is good news, or gospel, that we are healed, made whole, saved, and reconciled to God. This Gospel makes us children and ambassadors of God in His Kingdom. This is great news that we are the sons and daughters of God in His Kingdom which will reign forever and power on high has come upon us. This good news is that the Kingdom of God has been established and we have the keys to enter it and God has chosen to tabernacle in us.

This **sound doctrine** is what Paul was teaching. Paul taught not to deviate from this sound doctrine, although many will change it or try to change it, but Jesus said the gates of hell shall not prevail against His church.

This sound doctrine that Paul taught to the Ephesians is:

1. Believe in Jesus
2. Repent
3. Be baptized in the Name of Jesus
4. Since you are filled with His Holy Spirit, be holy
5. Rejoice!

Paul wraps up what we as believers in this sound doctrine are to do as members of the Body of Christ in Colossians 3:

Therefore, as God's chosen people, holy and dearly loved, clothe yourselves with compassion, kindness, humility, gentleness and patience. Bear with each other and forgive one another if any of you has a grievance against someone. Forgive as the Lord forgave you. And over all these virtues put on love, which binds them all together in perfect unity. Let the peace of Christ rule in your hearts, since as members of one body you were called to peace. And be thankful. Let the message of Christ dwell among you richly as you teach and admonish one another with all wisdom through psalms, hymns, and songs from the Spirit, singing to God with gratitude in your hearts. And whatever you do, whether in word or deed, do it all in the name of the Lord Jesus, giving thanks to God the Father through him (Colossians 3:12-17).

We are to love one another, as Christ loved the church.

Jesus Makes Us Real

Jesus makes us real, as we are dead in sin before becoming in Christ. The Bible teaches that through Christ, believers become new creations, truly alive in God's righteousness, and have Christ living within them, transforming their identity from spiritually dead to fully alive in Him, as seen in Ephesians 2:10, 2 Corinthians 5:17, and Galatians 2:20. These verses highlight becoming a "new self" or "new creation" in Christ, fulfilling God's purpose and reflecting His image.

Here are key verses that speak to this concept of Jesus making us real:

1. *For we are His workmanship, created in Christ Jesus for good works, which God prepared beforehand, that we should walk in them* (Ephesians 2:10).
2. *Therefore, if anyone is in Christ, he is a new creation. The old has passed away; behold, the new has come* (2 Corinthians 5:17).
3. *I have been crucified with Christ. It is no longer I who live, but Christ who lives in me. And the life I now live in the flesh I live by faith in the Son of God, who loved me and gave Himself for me* (Galatians 2:20).

4. *And to put on the new self, created after the likeness of God in true righteousness and holiness* (Ephesians 4:24).

In essence, Jesus makes us "real" by giving us a new, authentic identity as children of God, made alive through Him, fulfilling our true purpose, and indwelt by His Spirit, as explained in passages like Ephesians 2:4-5 and 1 Peter 1:23-25.

Love the Lord your God...

And one of the scribes came up and heard them disputing with one another, and seeing that he answered them well, asked him, "Which commandment is the most important of all?" Jesus answered, "The most important is, 'Hear, O Israel: The Lord our God, the Lord is one. And you shall love the Lord your God with all your heart and with all your soul and with all your mind and with all your strength.' The second is this: 'You shall love your neighbor as yourself.' There is no other commandment greater than these." And the scribe said to him, "You are right, Teacher. You have truly said that he is one, and there is no other besides him. And to love him with all the heart and with all the understanding and with all the strength, and to love one's neighbor as oneself, is much more than all whole burnt offerings and sacrifices." (Mark 12:28-33)

The scribes and Pharisees asked Jesus what was the greatest commandment. He answered quoting Deuteronomy 6:5:

Hear, O Israel: **The Lord our God, the Lord is One**. *And you shall love the Lord your God with all your heart and with all your soul and with all your mind and with all your strength.*

Love the Lord your God is a central biblical commandment, famously stated by Jesus in Matthew 22:37 as the first and greatest, meaning to love God with your entire being—heart, soul, and mind (or strength)—signifying total devotion, obedience, and a life-long, wholehearted relationship with Him, as emphasized in Deuteronomy 6:5 and Luke 10:27, forming the foundation of Christian faith and practice.

It is applied as total Commitment to God. It's a call for complete surrender and affection, engaging your emotions (heart), spiritual essence (soul), and intellect (mind/strength).

It is a foundation of faith. This love is the basis for all other commandments, including loving your neighbor.

This greatest of commandments is active and intentional. It's not passive; it involves actively seeking God, obeying His will, and living a life dedicated to Him, as seen in Deuteronomy 30:20:

Love *the LORD your God,* **obey Him,** *and* **remain faithful to Him**. *For He is your life, and He will prolong your life in the land the LORD swore to give to your fathers Abraham, Isaac, and Jacob* (Deuteronomy 30:20).

This greatest of commandments requires transformation. Loving God with the mind requires a renewed mind, which happens when sound doctrine is taught and applied and often achieved through understanding scripture and spiritual regeneration.

This commandment is of Biblically prophetic origin. The command echoes Old Testament scriptures like Deuteronomy 6:5 and Deuteronomy 10:12, repeated by prophets and Jesus.

In simple terms, the meaning of each is:

Heart: Your deepest affections and desires.

Soul: Your entire being, life, and inner self. Your mind, will, imagination, and emotions.

Mind/Strength: Your intellect, focus, and physical effort.

'Mind' which is added by both Jesus and the lawyer/scribe in the Scriptures is διάνοια, which has five uses:

1. the faculty of thinking, comprehending, and reasoning; understanding, intelligence, mind
2. mind as a mode of thinking, disposition, thoughts, mind
3. mind focused on objective, purpose, plan
4. mind as fantasizing power, imagination
5. mind in sensory aspect, power, impulse

The first is likely the meaning in both Luke and Matthew (also Mark 12:30). Yet, like love, there is a sense implying purposeful or focused action.

It means putting God first in every part of your life, loving Him more than anything else, and letting that love guide all your choices and actions.

Jesus then says:

*The second is this: 'You shall **love your neighbor** as yourself.' There is no other commandment greater than these.*

Jesus says the second great commandment is to love our neighbor. This is the hardest one. He describes the neighbor in the parable of the Good Samaritan, where even those you don't like and are different than you are the neighbor. He asks us to forgive those who have trespassed against us. He asks us to bless our enemies and pray for those who persecute us. That is because the new commandment that He has given us is to **love one another as He has loved us**. This is so important that in Matthew 24 the Lord explains that on this basis we will be judged:

*When the **Son of Man comes** in His glory, and all the angels with Him, He will sit on His glorious throne. All the nations will be gathered before Him, and He will separate the people one from another as a shepherd separates the sheep from the goats. He will put the sheep on His right and the goats on His left. "Then the King will say to those on his right, 'Come, you who are blessed by my Father; take your inheritance, the*

*kingdom prepared for you since the creation of the world. For **I was hungry and you gave me something to eat, I was thirsty and you gave me something to drink, I was a stranger and you invited me in, I needed clothes and you clothed me, I was sick and you looked after me, I was in prison and you came to visit me.'*
(Matthew 25:31-36).

So, we are to love God, our neighbor, **and ourselves**:

*The second is this: 'You shall love your neighbor **as yourself.'** There is no other commandment greater than these.*

If we don't love and take care of ourselves, we cannot love and care for our neighbors or minister to the Lord. Our bodies are the Temple of the Holy Spirit! As a church, the manifold wisdom of God, we are the Body of Christ! In order to love God and love our neighbor we have to love and take care of ourselves individually and ourselves as the Church.

Jesus Prayed for Us to be One:

*Holy Father, protect them by the **power of Your Name, the Name You gave Me**, so that they may be **one as We are one**... My prayer is not for them alone. I pray also for those who will believe in Me through their message, that **all of them may be one**, Father, just as You are in Me and I am in You. May they also be in Us so that the world may believe that You have sent Me. I have given them the glory that You gave Me, that **they may be one as We are one— I in them and You in Me**—so that they may be **brought to complete unity**.* (John 17:11; 20-23)

As Christians, we have taken on the Name of Christ. Christ prayed that we are one with Him as He and the Father are One. He prayed for all of us who believe, who have committed our life to Him and taken on His Name in covenant, to be one with Him. This is so that the world may believe by seeing the oneness we have with the Lord. Jesus also says that He has given us the glory that the Father gave Him, so that we may be one. This oneness with the Lord is so that we may be brought to complete unity. This is the same unity that Paul said the Lord left gifts for us to come into. Jesus loves His church, which is the manifold wisdom of God, in that He tabernacles within us.

I have made You known** to them, and will continue to make You known in order that the love you have for Me may be in them and that **I Myself may be in them (John 17:26).

Jesus finishes the prayer by saying that He has made God known to us and that He will be in us, His Body, and will be with us forever.

*And they continued steadfastly in the **apostles' doctrine** and fellowship, and in breaking of bread, and in prayers* (Acts 2:42).

The Church must devote themselves to apostolic doctrine, not early church father doctrine or denominational or academic doctrine, but specifically to what the apostles are teaching in the New Testament.

*Watch your life and **doctrine** closely. **Persevere** in them, because if you do, **you will save both yourself and your hearers*** (1 Timothy 4:16).

We must watch our lives closely and our doctrine closely, and persevere and remain in sound doctrine in order to save ourselves and those that hear the message of the Kingdom of God. How can our doctrine give us salvation or those who hear us teach receive salvation from our doctrine? It is the doctrine that heals, reconciles, and saves us by obedience to the Lord through belief and faith in Jesus, repentance, baptism in the Name of Jesus, and the infilling of the Spirit of God that brings us into the eternal Kingdom of God. This is the doctrine that Peter and the apostles taught on the Day of Pentecost in Acts 2, the doctrine that Jesus taught in the Gospels and when He instructed Ananias what to teach Paul, and the sound doctrine that Paul taught at Ephesus in the book of Acts and that he was charging and reminding Timothy to do as overseer of Ephesus.

Sound Doctrine Leads to Worship

We were created to worship and praise God. Several Scriptures reveal that He created all things for His pleasure, formed to show forth His praise, and describing believers as a people called to proclaim His excellencies.

Worthy are you, our Lord and God, to receive glory and honor *and power, for you created all things, and by your will they existed and were created* (Revelation 4:11).

The people whom I formed for Myself **that they might declare My praise** (Isaiah 43:21).

But you are a chosen people, a royal priesthood, a holy nation, God's special possession, **that you may declare the praises of Him** *who called you out of darkness into His wonderful light* (1 Peter 2:9).

For by Him all things were created, in heaven and on earth, visible and invisible... all things were created through Him and **for Him** (Colossians 1:16).

These verses illuminate that our purpose is to glorify God through worship and praise. They suggest that worship isn't just an activity but the very reason for creation and our existence. The focus is on declaring God's greatness and showing forth His praise through our lives, works, and worship.

The Psalmist writes that praise erupts from the study of God's works:

Praise *the Lord! I will give* **thanks** *to the Lord with my whole heart, in the company of the upright, in the congregation.* **Great are the works of the Lord, <u>studied by all who delight in them</u>**. *Full of splendor and majesty is His work, and His righteousness endures forever. He has caused His wondrous works to be remembered; the Lord is gracious and merciful. He provides food for those who fear Him; He remembers His covenant forever. He has shown His people the power of His works, in giving them the inheritance of the nations. The works of His hands are faithful and just; all His precepts are trustworthy; they are established forever and ever, to be* *performed with faithfulness and uprightness. He sent redemption to His people; He has commanded His covenant forever.* **Holy and awesome is His name!** *The fear of the Lord is the beginning of wisdom; all those who practice it have a good understanding.* **His praise endures forever!** (Psalm 111:1-9)

What are David and the worshiper of God to study? The works of the Lord that are preserved in His Word as sound doctrine!

Many scholars will agree that Romans is one of the greatest books ever written. The latter end of Romans from chapters 9 to 11 are some of the deepest theological doctrine written. At the end of Romans 11, after writing this, Paul praises God with the following doxology:

Oh, the depth of the riches of the wisdom and knowledge of God! How unsearchable His judgments, and His paths beyond tracing out! Who has known the mind of the Lord? Or who has been His counselor? Who has ever given to God, that God should repay them? For from Him and through Him and for Him are all things. To Him be the glory forever! Amen. (Romans 11:33-36)

What moved Paul from deep theological writing to worship? In the context of these verses, the answer is obvious: **doctrine**. Doctrine motivated him to ecstasy and worship. His doctrine erupted into magnificent worship! We study God and sound doctrine to praise God! Our doctrine leads to worship! And we cannot praise what we do not know. The study of God is practical for our lives and sound doctrine is necessary for eternity!

† Biography

Dr. Les Moore served as overseer and senior pastor of Wellspring Church in Clifton Springs, New York, and as senior pastor of Clifton Spa Chapel. He has served professionally for thirty years as a pastoral counselor, providing pastoral and spiritual care and counseling in a clinical setting. Dr. Moore has a Master of Art in Applied Theology and a three-year graduate Certificate in Pastoral Care and Counseling from Marylhurst University and a Doctor of Ministry in Practical Theology from Wagner University. Dr. Moore served as an airborne infantry soldier, sergeant, and officer in various assignments in motorized, mechanized, and light infantry units, including with 1st Recondo, 9th Infantry Division (Motorized); Spartan Battalion, 36th Infantry Regiment, 3rd Armored Division; and 187th Rakkasan Regiment, 101st Airborne Division. He practices as a naturopathic doctor and acupuncturist in Fairport, NY and served on the National Park System Advisory Board, appointed by the Secretary of the Interior, and served as an advisor to the Secretary of the Interior and the National Park Service Director. He was the Co-Chair of Workforce Planning for the National Park Service, Chair of the Committee on Health, Wellness, and Safety, and Chair of the Tourism Committee and Tourism Workgroup for the National Park Service and has served under two presidents and three secretaries. He previously served for ten years under four governors on the Board for Professional Medical Conduct in New York Office of Professional Medical Conduct and served as the Director of

Integrative Medicine for twelve years at Clifton Springs Hospital and Clinic in Clifton Springs, New York, and prior to that at FF Thompson Hospital in Canandaigua, New York.

Made in the USA
Middletown, DE
24 February 2026